REFLECTIONS OF A
SOLDIER AND SERVANT

REFLECTIONS OF A
SOLDIER AND SERVANT

F. DEAN NEMECEK

Pleasant Word

ISBN 13: 978-1-4141-1185-8
ISBN 10: 1-4141-1185-1
Library of Congress Catalog Card Number: 2008900609

ACKNOWLEDGMENTS

I want to express sincere thanks to Amy Nemecek, wife of my grandson Sean. A busy mother and pastor's wife, Amy spent a lot of time copyediting and preparing this book for print publication. Dean would be so proud of her, as he was of all his children and grandchildren.

I also want to thank my sons, Stephen and Paul, for suggestions they made as I finished organizing the book after Dean's death. Thank you, as well, to the many friends and family members who sent letters or emails and who called or visited, encouraging Dean to keep writing devotionals during his years of illness and suggesting that he put them into a book so that others could enjoy them.

—Sylvia Nemecek

ABOUT THE AUTHOR

Rev. F. Dean Nemecek was a soldier, an educator, and a minister of the gospel of Jesus Christ. He served in World War II from November 1943 until April 1946. Dean was in the 379th Regiment of the 100th Infantry Division in the mortar section where he was awarded the Bronze Star for Meritorious Service.

Upon his return from service, Dean earned his B.A. at Coe College in Cedar Rapids, Iowa, the city where he had been born. After his marriage in 1949 he entered Northern Baptist Seminary and earned his B.D. degree. He served churches in Rockford and Chicago, Illinois, as well as Oscoda, Michigan, while continuing his education, earning a M.S. at Northern Illinois University and a Ph.D. at Loyola University. During this time he also served as an adjunct professor for Wheaton College.

Dean and his wife, Sylvia, and their four children moved to Rochester, New York, in 1970 when he accepted the position of Dean of Students at Roberts Wesleyan College. He served as the dean, as well as teaching several courses, over the next eleven years. He was highly thought of by faculty and students alike. The 1975 yearbook, *Chesbronian*, was dedicated to him. Upon leaving Roberts, Dean served a church in Lincoln, New York, and worked for New York State as a chaplain at Craig Development Center in Sonyea, NY, and later in their group homes.

He retired in 1988 and in his retirement years served thirteen times as interim pastor in churches in western New York, serving two churches twice. He had been blessed with good health all his years, but in 2004 as he approached his 79th birthday, he was suddenly diagnosed with severe osteoporosis and a form of cancer known as multiple myeloma. At the same time several other ailments were diagnosed, making it very difficult for him to breathe. After a very active life, he was suddenly pretty much housebound and on oxygen around the clock. However, he continued to serve the Lord that he loved by writing a devotional each week. He could no longer sit at the computer and type, but would write them out in longhand and his wife would type them. These were sent out via email to all his children, grandchildren, and other members of his extended family.

Soon friends from the several churches that he had served, as well as other friends, asked to be put on his email list. He faithfully sent out a devotional every week until the day of his death in October 2007. Many of the recipients forwarded them to others. Dean received emails, letters, and visits from people that he had not known, as well as those that he did. They told him how they had been blessed by a particular devotional. Many of those who received them asked that they be put into a book. This book is offered in response to those requests.

THE LISTENING POST

The Lord came and stood there, calling as at the other times, "Samuel! Samuel!" Then Samuel said, "Speak, for your servant is listening."
—1 Samuel 3:10 NIV

E. Stanley Jones, missionary to India, conference speaker, and devotional writer observed what he called his "Listening Post." Each morning before he did anything else, he would get up, sit in a chair and ask, "Lord, what is it that you have to say to me today?" Inevitably he received an answer to his question giving him guidance for the day. Some days he got real surprised. One morning he got up and asked, "Lord, what is it that you have to say to me today?"

The Lord seemed to be saying, "Stanley, you're tired. Go back to bed." So Stanley went back to bed!

When you pray, don't give God orders. Just report for duty.

"Speak; for thy servant heareth" (1 Sam. 3:10).

DON'T HAVE A GOOD DAY

I have learned to be content with whatever I have.

—Philippians 4:11 NRSV

Alta Brush was a ninety-four-year-old resident of the Fairport Baptist Homes in Rochester, New York. She was confined to her bed and wheelchair. Her mind, however, was clear as could be. She had been a member of the Lincoln Baptist Church where I served as pastor. Each week as I drove to the church I would stop at the Home to visit Mrs. Brush. I always found her bright and cheery. I also noticed that anytime that a staff member came into the room while I was there, that the person invariably commented on what a good patient Mrs. Brush was. I do know that she always managed to cheer me up.

One day as I was leaving after our weekly visit, I paused in the doorway and waved to her. "Have a good day," I said. She looked at me with a rather stern expression and replied, "Your day is what you make it." That response explained a great deal about Alta Brush. It was, whether she realized it or not, her philosophy of life.

As I drove away from the Home that day I could not help but think of those words of the apostle Paul written from his Roman prison cell, "I have learned to be content with whatever I have" (Phil. 4:11). That explains why Paul could also say to the Philippian church, "Rejoice in the Lord always; again I will say, rejoice" (4:4).

Don't have a good day. Make a good day.

THE PRODIGAL PUPPY

There is rejoicing in the presence of the angels of God over one sinner who repents.

—Luke 15:10b NIV

Our newlywed neighbors brought a puppy with them when they moved in next door. His name is "Radar." The reason that his owners named him Radar, I think, is because he has one ear that always sticks up like a radar antenna. Both of Radar's owners work during the day. They didn't want to leave him tied up all day and they didn't want to leave him alone in the house all day either, so they installed an invisible fence. The invisible fence is simply an electrical cable buried underground. The dog wears a little box on his collar. If he comes too close to the cable the box gives the dog an electrical shock. It sounds cruel, but the dog soon learns not to go near the invisible fence.

Of course, the invisible fence does not prevent other animals or people from entering the yard. That was alright, too. A couple of little girls who live across the street would come often and play with Radar. Occasionally, another dog would come in the yard and Radar would have another playmate. One day a big dog from the neighborhood came into Radar's yard. The two dogs had a great time together; running around the yard chasing each other. Finally, the big dog decided to move on. He simply crossed the invisible fence without harm, of course. Radar, forgetting about the invisible fence, followed his new friend across the barrier. He received a shock and just stood there outside of the fence very bewildered. The other dog trotted away leaving Radar behind. Well, the invisible fence works both ways. Radar could not get back into his own yard without receiving a shock and he seemed quite reluctant to do so. He was looking pretty dejected. His food and water and his nice warm bed were on the other side of the invisible fence.

God's rules are like that invisible fence. They are for our good. They keep us in God's love and care. When we disobey God's rules, we find ourselves separated from God and very miserable.

When I saw poor Radar in his dilemma, I knew exactly what to do. You see, each day after she returns from school his mistress, who is a teacher, takes Radar for a walk. The way that she gets him through the invisible fence is to pick him up and carry him across. Her body shields the puppy from the electrical shock. So that's what I did. I picked little Radar up and carried him across the invisible fence and set him down in his own yard. Let me tell you that he was one happy puppy. You see, when we break God's laws and find ourselves separated from Him, He finds us and picks us up in His arms and carries us back home where we belong.

KEEPING UP WITH THE JONESES

Godliness with contentment is great gain.

—1 Timothy 6:6 NIV

I like the story about the man who came unexpectedly into a considerable fortune but nevertheless continued to live in the same old house in the same old neighborhood. One of his friends was curious about that and asked him one day, "Why do you stay here when you can afford to buy a big house in a ritzy neighborhood?"

The fellow answered his friend, "Well, I'll tell you. You have heard of keeping up with the Joneses, haven't you? Well, here I'm Jones."

Keeping up with the Joneses seems to be part of the American way of life. I saw a sign once in a hardware store that put it well. It read, "Isn't it strange that we spend money that we haven't got to buy things that we don't need to impress people that we don't like."

There are many warnings in Scripture about the deceitfulness of riches. We are told that "The love of money is the root of all evil" (1 Tim. 6:10). Jesus admonished, "Lay not up for yourselves treasures upon earth, where moth and rust doth corrupt and where thieves break through and steal: but lay up for yourselves treasures in heaven, where neither moth nor rust doth corrupt, and where thieves do not break through nor steal" (Matt. 6:19-20).

The apostle Paul put things in proper perspective when he wrote to Timothy, "We brought nothing into this world, and it is certain we can carry nothing out. Therefore, having food and clothing let us be content" (1 Tim. 6:7-8). After Henry Thoreau had spent a year beside Walden Pond living off the land he made this observation, "A man is rich in proportion to the number of things that he can afford to do without."

ENJOYING THE STRUGGLE

Consider it pure joy whenever you face trials of many kinds, because you know that the testing of your faith develops perseverance.
—James 1:2-3 NIV

One day when I was in my early teens, I was visiting in the home of my aunt Florence in Cedar Rapids, Iowa. I was listening to a conversation between Aunt Florence and her daughter, Norma, my cousin about the same age as I. Norma was bemoaning the injustice of life. She said, "Life isn't fair. You work hard all your life to earn enough money to enjoy life, but when you do get enough money, you're too old to enjoy it."

I'll never forget Aunt Florence's reply. "Well, dear, you just have to learn to enjoy the struggle."

Aunt Florence lived to be ninety-two. When she was ninety she suffered a stroke and was never able to walk or talk again. She was taken to live with her son in Arkansas. Each morning she would be wheeled out onto the patio where she took great delight in watching the little birds at the feeder. You just have to learn to enjoy the struggle.

"Consider it pure joy whenever you face trials of many kinds, because you know that the testing of your faith develops perseverance" (James 1:2 NIV).

THE DEVIL MADE ME DO IT

Resist the devil and he will flee from you.

—James 4:7b NIV

One of the highlights of my three years at Northern Baptist Theological Seminary was a series of lectures by Dr. Andrew Blackwood, professor of preaching at Princeton Theological Seminary and author of several classic works on preaching. I have benefited greatly over the years from Dr. Blackwood's books.

Oddly enough, the thing that I remember most about his visit to the Northern campus was a story about Albert Einstein that Dr. Blackwood told in one of my classes. The Einsteins and the Blackwoods were next-door neighbors in Princeton. One day in the early years of Hitler's rise to power Dr. Einstein and Mrs. Blackwood were talking over the back fence about the situation in Europe. Mrs. Blackwood asked, "What do you think is the matter with that Hitler fellow?"

Dr. Einstein replied, "Oh, a case of glands."

Somehow that didn't quite fit with Mrs. Blackwood's Presbyterian theology and so she answered, "Well, personally I think it's the devil."

Einstein responded dryly, "Same thing, same thing."

It is a very common tendency to account for human behavior on the basis of factors other than personal choice. This tendency has a long history. In fact, it goes all the way back to the Garden of Eden when Adam passed the buck saying, "The woman gave me of the tree and I did eat" (Gen. 3:12). We often hear explanations for human behavior on the basis of heredity and/or environment. While these factors should never be discounted, the truth is that ultimately we are what we choose to be. All law, morality, and religion is based on the assumption of personal responsibility. I like the way one candidate for ordination explained the doctrine of election, which we sometimes call predestination. He really didn't know what it meant so he tried to fake it. He said, "The doctrine of election means that the Lord casts a vote for you, the devil casts a vote for you, and you cast the deciding vote."

OLD HABITS DIE HARD

For what I do is not the good I want to do; no, the evil I do not want to do—this I keep on doing.

—Romans 7:19 NIV

For a few months following the end of World War II in Europe I lived in the lovely little village of Ditzigen, a suburb of Stuttgart, Germany. Unlike the city of Stuttgart itself which had been nearly leveled to the ground by American bombers, Ditzigen had suffered little physical damage. However, the people of the village shared with the rest of the nation in much deprivation caused by the war, particularly the shortage of food. At mealtime the children of the village would come to the inn that served as our mess hall and stand outside with their buckets waiting for the soldiers to come out and give them the uneaten food on their plates.

After a few days the children and the GIs became increasingly friendly. The children would come early at mealtime and try to talk to the soldiers waiting in line for the mess hall to open. One morning a sleepy-eyed little boy, perhaps eight or nine years old, came up to the men waiting in the chow line and greeted them with the salutation which he had used almost all of his life: "Heil Hitler."

No sooner were the words out of his mouth than he realized that he had made a horrible blunder. The expression on his face reflected the terror in his heart. He was certain, I am sure, that he was about to be arrested or beaten. Imagine the relief that he felt when the GIs, to a man, instead roared with laughter. I was very proud to be an American at that moment.

There are many warnings in Scripture against the human tendency to return to our old ways after having seen the light of God. Moses chastised the children of Israel, for after having been delivered from the bondage of Egypt, they longed for the leeks and wild garlic of that country. Lot's wife, who was saved from the destruction of Sodom and Gomorrah, looked back and was turned into a pillar of salt. Jesus said, "No man, having put his hand to the plough and looking back, is fit for the kingdom of God" (Luke 9:62). The apostle Paul described those who receive Christ and then return to their former way of life as a dog returning to this vomit.

All of this is pretty discouraging for those of us who so often fail and fall. However, we must remember the words of St. Augustine, "There is nothing sweeter than coming to Christ, unless it is coming to him again." The apostle Peter denied the Lord three times in one night. Later, in a beautiful scene beside the Sea of Galilee, Jesus offered Peter threefold forgiveness. Jesus said that we should forgive our brother as often as seventy times seven. If that can be true of human beings, then how much more true of the God of all grace.

IF YOU CAN'T STAND THE HEAT

Humble yourselves under the mighty hand of God.

—1 Peter 5:6b NKJV

It was a hot, muggy day in Rockford, Illinois as I made my pastoral rounds. Visiting in the home of a dear Swedish lady I commented on the oppressive weather. She replied, "And it isn't just the heat. It's the humility." I am sure that she meant humidity. I suppose that the proper thing to do was to correct her, but I had such a difficult time keeping a straight face that I couldn't do so.

Later that day, back in my study at the church, I thought again about that incident. After another chuckle to myself it suddenly occurred to me that there was a profound hidden truth in the lady's statement. Our attitude toward the weather can make a difference in our ability to cope with it. Peter Marshall ministered in Washington, DC during the years of World War II when there was no air conditioning available. He often prayed from the pulpit of the New York Avenue Presbyterian Church thanking God that there is no weather in heaven.

What is true of the weather is true also of the trials and tribulations of life in general. Our attitude makes all the difference in the world. As someone has said, "It doesn't make any difference how great the pressure is from the outside as long as the pressure from the inside is equal to it." It does make a difference when you can say with the apostle Paul, "I consider that the sufferings of this present time are not worth comparing with the glory that is to be revealed to us" (Rom. 8:18 RSV). Or, "We know that in everything God works for good with those who love Him, who are called according to His purpose" (Rom. 8:28 RSV).

Popular wisdom says, "If you can't stand the heat, get out of the kitchen." The Bible says, "If you can't stand the heat, try humility."

"Humble yourselves under the mighty hand of God, that in due time he may exalt you. Cast all your anxieties on Him, for he cares for you" (1 Peter 5:6-7).

WIVES, SUBMIT YOURSELVES TO YOUR HUSBANDS

Wives, submit to your husbands as to the Lord.

—Ephesians 5:22 NIV

There are those who interpret these words of the apostle Paul from Ephesians 5:22 to mean that the husband is to be the monarch of all that he surveys and his wife is to be only his humble and obedient servant. I think of an episode from *The Honeymooners*. Ralph Cramden and his wife Alice are having a heated argument.

Ralph says, "Remember, I'm the boss. You're nothing."

To this Alice replies, "Big deal. You're the boss of nothing."

So much for the macho man view of marriage.

There are those who teach that Christianity gave women an inferior role in society. As a matter of fact, Christianity exalted women to a place that they had never before had in the ancient world and no religion or philosophy since has given women a higher place than has true Christian teaching. This passage clearly demonstrates that. Before Paul says, "Wives, submit yourselves unto your own husbands," he says that husbands and wives are to submit themselves to each other, for we read in verse 21 of Ephesians 5, "Submit yourselves one to another out of reverence for Christ." In other words, husbands and wives are to be equal partners in a Christian marriage. As St. Augustine put it, "God did not take woman out of the head of man that she might be above him or out of the feet of man that she might be beneath him but out of the side of man that they might be equals." I think that Charles E. Fuller of the Old Fashioned Revival Hour was nearer the truth of this passage when he said that marriage is not a fifty/fifty proposition but must be at least a sixty/forty one if it is to succeed. That is, each partner must be willing to go more than halfway to meet the other if the marriage is to be a happy one. That's what Paul meant when he said, "Submit to one another out of reverence for Christ" (Eph. 5:21 NIV).

17

SUFFICIENT GRACE

And He [Jesus] said unto me, "My grace is sufficient for thee: for my strength is made perfect in weakness." Most gladly therefore will I rather glory in my infirmities, that the power of Christ may rest upon me.
—2 Corinthians 12:9

In her famous devotional classic *Streams in the Desert*, Mrs. Charles Cowman tells of a minister who was grieving over the death of one of his children when he saw a plaque containing the words of 2 Corinthians 12:9, "My grace is sufficient for thee." He noted that the word "is" was painted bright green to make it stand out from the other words. He immediately understood the message. My grace is (not shall be or may be) sufficient for thee. God cannot make His grace any more sufficient that He has already made it; get up and believe it and you will find it to be true.

Whenever I think of this verse I am reminded of the life and ministry of Dr. Everett Swanson, founder of Compassion, a ministry to Korean orphans. Rev. Swanson was the very successful pastor of a large Baptist church on Chicago's west side in spite of the fact that he had never attended college or seminary. At the height of his pastoral career he felt that God was calling him to become an itinerant evangelist. He resigned his church to devote himself to his new calling. The first series of meetings that he held was in my church in Rockford, Illinois. He asked me if he could receive an offering at one of the meetings for some Korean orphans. As far as I know that was the first public offering received for what was to become a multimillion dollar missionary organization. In appreciation of his work with orphans Mr. Swanson received an honorary doctorate from the University of Seoul and in addition the highest award given by the South Korean government. Unfortunately, Rev. Swanson died of cancer in his mid-fifties.

When I learned of Everett's illness I recalled an incident from those meetings in Rockford years earlier. One evening Rev. Swanson and his wife sang a duet in the service. They sang of the riches of God's grace.

> He giveth more grace when the burdens grow greater.
> He sendeth more strength when the labors increase.
> To added affliction He addeth his mercies,
> To multiplied trials His multiplied peace.
>
> When we have exhausted our store of endurance
> When our strength has failed ere the day is half done,
> When we reach the end of our hoarded resources
> Our Father's full giving is only begun.
>
> His love has no limit, His grace has no measure,
> His power no boundary known unto men;
> For out of His infinite riches in Jesus
> He giveth and giveth and giveth again.
> (Annie Johnson Flint, "He Giveth More Grace")

"My grace IS sufficient for thee."

THE NAME OF JESUS

And whatever you do, whether in word or deed, do it all in the name of the Lord Jesus.

—Colossians 3:17 NIV

One morning when I was serving my first church back in Rockford, Illinois, I received a call from a mother whose daughter was enrolled in the Junior Girls Class of our Sunday school. She said, "Pastor, I have a question to ask you. Who is Yesus? Every Sunday my little girl comes home from Sunday school and all she talks about all week long is Yesus. Who is Yesus?"

I will admit that I had to laugh a bit before I could answer. Then I went on to explain to that mother that the teacher of the class, Annie Aldeen, had come to this country from Sweden when she was a teenager and that she had a Swedish accent. There is no "J" sound in Swedish, so every word starting with "J" comes out as a "Y." So Yesus is Jesus. I think that that mother was quite relieved to know that her daughter was not involved with some kind of a cult.

As I hung up the phone I could not help but give thanks for that teacher who shared with those girls so effectively the joy of the Lord in her heart and life that they talked about nothing else but Jesus all week long. Oh that there were more Christians like that!

Yes, it is true. A rose by any other name would smell as sweet.

How sweet the name of Jesus sounds
In a believer's ear!
It soothes his sorrows, heals his wounds,
And drives away his fear.

Jesus, my Shepherd, Brother, Friend,
My Prophet, Priest and King,
My Lord, my Life, my Way, my End,
Accept the praise I bring.
　　　(John Newton, "How Sweet The Name of Jesus Sounds")

THE TEST

No temptation has seized you except what is common to man. And God is faithful; He will not let you be tempted beyond what you can bear. But when you are tempted, He will also provide a way out so that you can stand up under it.

—1 Corinthians 10:13 NIV

Nell was a recent nursing school graduate. She was employed as an operating room nurse in a large hospital. She enjoyed her work and was good at it. She seemed to have a promising future.

Something puzzled her though. Several of the other operating room nurses had warned her, "Watch out for Dr. X!" When she asked why, she always got the same answer, "You'll find out."

Finally, the day came to work with Dr. X. Everything went well until it came time to account for the gauze pads used during the surgery. According to Nell there was one missing. Dr. X insisted that Nell had miscounted. She counted them again with the same result—there was a gauze pad missing. The doctor still insisted that she had made a mistake and said that he was going to close up. Nell said, "I'm sorry, Doctor, but I'll have to call my supervisor."

"You don't have to do that," the doctor said. "Look at my foot." He moved his foot and there was the missing pad. He had been standing on it. This was the trick that Dr. X played on each new nurse. He wanted to see if the nurse would stand up for her conviction or buckle under the authority of the surgeon. Nell had passed the test. She and Dr. X remained good friends for many years. Many times God allows our faith to be tested. He permitted his own Son to be tempted by Satan in the wilderness for forty days. It is important to notice that the gospel says that Jesus was led by the Spirit into the wilderness where He was tempted.

Temptation can take many forms. John speaks of "the lust of the flesh, and the lust of the eyes, and the pride of life" (1 John 2:16). Paul reminds us, "but God is faithful, who will not suffer you to be tempted above that ye are able; but will with the temptation also make a way to escape, that ye may be able to bear it" (1 Cor. 10:13).

THE HEALING TOUCH

Jesus reached out his hand and touched the man.

—Matthew 8:3a NIV

One of the miracles of Jesus that has always intrigued me is the healing of a leper. In response to the man's plea, Jesus reached forth and touched him and the man was made whole. The miracle itself is amazing enough, but to think that Jesus touched the leper is absolutely astounding. In the first place, it was against the Mosaic law to touch a leper, so that Jesus became ceremonially unclean by touching the man. And, of course, there was the possibility of contracting the disease.

Touching the leper seemed to be instrumental in his healing. A few years ago there was a report in the *New England Journal of Medicine* that indicated that doctors who made a practice of touching their patients in the hospital were more successful than those who did not. Those who were touched had shorter stays in the hospital than the other group.

In recent years a number of pop psychologists have pointed out the fact that we all have the healing touch. We all have the power to comfort, strengthen, and encourage others by reaching out to them physically as well as emotionally.

There is a beautiful story about Henry Drummond, the author of *The Greatest Thing in the World*. The little pamphlet is an exposition of 1 Corinthians 13, the Love Chapter of the Bible. A young man presented himself for membership in a church in England. He explained that he had been converted to Christ through the influence of Henry Drummond. At the mention of that famous name the elders became quite interested. One of them asked, "What was it that Dr. Drummond said that caused you to be converted?" The young man said, "Well, he didn't say anything. He just put his hand on my shoulder."

When a man ain't got a friend and is feeling kinda blue,
And the clouds hang low and heavy and won't let the sunshine
through;
'Tis a great thing, oh my brother, for a fellow just to lay
His hand upon your shoulder in a friendly sort of way.

Now this world's a curious compound with its honey and its gall,
With its cares and bitter crosses; but a good world after all.
And a good God must have made it, least wise that is what I say,
When His hand is on my shoulder in a friendly sort of way.

DOES GOD MAKE IT RAIN?

And we know that all things work together for good to those who love
God, to those who are the called according to His purpose.
—Romans 8:28 NKJV

I was sitting in a pavilion in the park with my five-year-old grand-daughter watching it rain. Our family had come to the park expecting to spend the day enjoying a picnic lunch and the beauty of the park and, of course, the playground. Unfortunately, the rain disrupted our plans. While we were sitting in the pavilion, my granddaughter asked, "Does God make it rain?"

I could see that I needed to be careful how I answered the question, but I wanted to be honest so I said, "Yes, God makes it rain."

I was not as prepared, however, for my granddaughter's response. She said, "I hate God." Oops!

I tried to explain that even though our picnic was disrupted by the rain, the rain was nevertheless a good thing. After all, the things that made the park such a beautiful place—the trees, the grass, the flowers, the waterfalls—were all there because of rain. She seemed to understand and agree but at the same time I sensed that in the back of her mind was the response of Brother Juniper, the cartoon character monk. "I know it's His rain, but it's our picnic."

Romans 8:28 was a favorite verse of John Foster Dulles, Secretary of State in the Eisenhower administration. "We know that all things work together for good to those who love God, to those who are called according to His purpose." He said that when things were going badly in the Cold War that he would go off by himself and meditate on this verse, attempting to discover where his purposes were contrary to God's.

"Trust in the LORD with all your heart, and lean not unto your own understanding; in all your ways acknowledge Him and He shall direct your paths" (Prov. 3:5-6 NKJV).

GOING THE SECOND MILE

Whoever compels you to go one mile, go with him two.
—Matthew 5:41 NKJV

When our family moved to Rochester in July, 1970, Sylvia was completing work on a master's degree at Northeastern Illinois University in Chicago and so remained behind with our two oldest boys. Since we had only one car and my office at Roberts Wesleyan College was just two blocks from our house in North Chili, we agreed that she should have the car.

That worked out just fine until the first Saturday morning when I decided to do some grocery shopping. The Super-Duper in North Chili is several blocks from the house where we lived, so I decided to ride a bicycle. At the store I bought two bags of groceries and a watermelon. Now I don't know if you have ever seen a man ride a bicycle carrying two bags of groceries and a watermelon, but I can assure you that it is quite a trick. I did alright until I turned off Buffalo Road onto College Drive where our house was located. There is a deep drainage ditch there. I cut the corner a little short and ended up at the bottom of the drainage ditch beneath the bicycle, two bags of groceries, and the watermelon.

This all happened right across the street from the Pearce Memorial Free Methodist parsonage. Rev. Elwyn Cutler, the senior pastor, happened to be looking out the window at the time. He rushed out of the house, picked me up, and helped retrieve the groceries. He helped carry the groceries to our house down the block and into the kitchen. As he turned to leave, he said, "Now, Dean, we have two cars at our house. My wife doesn't work on Saturday, so I will leave our second car in the driveway with the key in it, so you can just help yourself any Saturday." I thanked him, of course.

Somehow, however, he sensed that I was not likely to come and take the car on my own, because the next Saturday when I woke up, there was his car parked in my driveway. That is what I call going the second mile. It has been over thirty-five years since this incident. Rev. Cutler had a very successful career as the senior pastor of Pearce Memorial Church, one of the largest Protestant congregations in Rochester. He was a good preacher, a good pastor, and a good administrator. He went from the Pearce church to become crusade coordinator for Billy Graham and had a distinguished career there as well. But as for me, I will always remember him for this simple act of kindness performed in July, 1970.

GO FLY A KITE

Now faith is the substance of things hoped for, the evidence of things not seen.

—Hebrews 11:1

A man walking through a park noticed a boy flying a kite. At least that is what he thought the boy was doing because the kite was behind a cloud so that all that could be seen from the ground was a boy holding onto a string dangling from the sky. The man thought that he would have a little fun with the boy and so asked him, "What are you doing?"

The boy replied, "I'm flying my kite."

"I don't see any kite," the man persisted. "How do you know that there is a kite up there?"

The boy answered, "Every once in awhile the kite gives a little tug on the string so that I know it's still there."

That little tug is called faith. The Bible defines faith as "the evidence of things not seen." Faith is that state of mind in which the things that are not seen become as real as those which are seen. Emily Dickinson spoke of this faith in *Chartless*:

I never saw the moor; I never saw the sea;
Yet, know I how the heather looks and what a wave must be.
I never spoke with God or visited in heaven;
Yet, certain am I of the spot as though a chart were given.

How does one "get" faith? For "without faith it is impossible to please God" (Heb. 11:6). If you have ever flown a kite perhaps you remember that when you pull on the string there is a responding tug from the kite. The Bible says, "Call upon me and I will answer you and show you great and mighty things" (Jer. 33:3). "We walk by faith, not by sight" (2 Cor. 5:7).

AAA

O

You therefore must endure hardship as a good soldier of Jesus Christ.
—2 Timothy 2:3 NKJV

In his memoirs of World War II, *A Soldier's Story*, General Omar Bradley tells of an incident that occurred during the early days of the fighting in North Africa. General Bradley had been chosen by General Eisenhower to act as Eisenhower's "eyes and ears" at the front. One day General Bradley was traveling through territory occupied by one of the regiments of the First Infantry Division, "The Big Red One." Everywhere he went he saw this strange marking: AAA, beneath that a line, and beneath the line a zero. He saw it on tanks, trucks, jeeps, helmets, and more: AAA, beneath that a line, and beneath the line a zero. He was somewhat concerned since he didn't recognize that as any kind of official marking and it was against regulations to put special markings on government equipment.

Finally, he came across Colonel Paddy Flint, the commander of that regiment and an old professional soldier like himself. Bradley asked, "Paddy, what is this that I see everywhere I go in your outfit, AAA line zero? What does that mean?"

Colonel Flint drew himself up proudly and said, "Sir, that means anything, anytime, anywhere, bar nothing."

Those words take on added significance when we remember that Paddy Flint was killed in the invasion of Normandy. Anything, anytime, anywhere, bar nothing; what a motto for a soldier! And what a motto for a soldier of the cross! Anything, anytime, anywhere, bar nothing for Jesus Christ. "Greater love has no man than this, that a man lay down his life for his friends" (John 15:13 RSV).

THE BROWN BAG LUNCH

Give thanks in all circumstances, for this is God's will for you in Christ Jesus.

—1 Thessalonians 5:18 NIV

Mark worked as a caretaker on one of those beautiful estates that line the shores of some of the Finger Lakes in Western New York. One day he was sitting at the end of the pier at the estate eating his brown bag lunch. He was feeling pretty low. He was forty years old, had no family, was not in the best of health, and didn't appear to have much of a future.

The five-year-old granddaughter of the owners of the estate saw Mark, walked up to him eating his brown bag lunch at the end of the pier, and asked him in the sweetest little voice, "Are you having a picnic?" Mark said that it was just as if the sun had broken through a dark cloud. The whole world looked different for now he was seeing it through the wondering eyes of a little child.

It's true. One man's brown bag lunch is another man's picnic. When Sylvia was in school her mother baked bread for her school lunches. However, Sylvia preferred "store-bought bread" so would trade her sandwich for someone else's with "store-bought bread." Sometimes she would get two or three offers and could choose the best.

When upon life's billows you are tempest tossed,
When you are discouraged thinking all is lost;
Count your many blessings; name them one by one,
And it will surprise you what the Lord has done.
(Johnson Oatman, Jr., "Count Your Blessings")

"Rejoice in the Lord always and again I say, rejoice" (Phil. 4:4).

THANKS TO GOD

Give thanks to the LORD, for He is good; His love endures forever.
—Psalm 106:1b NIV

Herb Skoglund, a retired pharmacist, was a member of our congregation in Chicago. In his late seventies he developed Parkinson's disease and after several months in a private hospital entered Hines Veteran's Hospital where he would die a few weeks later. I visited Herb the first day that he was at Hines and was with him when his first meal was brought to him. When his tray was placed in front of him, he bowed his head, closed his eyes, and began to pray aloud, completely oblivious to the other people in the room. "Thank you, Jesus," he began. That may have seemed a strange prayer to some for there was little to be thankful for. But thanksgiving was the lifelong habit of this wonderful Christian man, and some things had not changed. As I drove away from the hospital later that day, the words of an old Swedish hymn ran through my mind.

Thanks to God for my redeemer,
Thanks for all Thou dost provide!
Thanks for times but now a memory,
Thanks for Jesus by my side.

Thanks for pleasant, balmy springtime,
Thanks for dark and dreary fall!
Thanks for tears by now forgotten.
Thanks for peace within my soul!

Thanks for prayers that Thou hast answered,
Thanks for what Thou dost deny!

Thanks for storms that I have weathered,
Thanks for all Thou dost supply!

Thanks for pain and thanks for pleasure,
Thanks for comfort in despair,
Thanks for grace that none can measure,
Thanks for love beyond compare!
       (A. L. Storm, "Thanks to God," trans. C. E. Backstrom)

Thanks be unto God for His unspeakable gift!

THE WORLD'S MOST UNUSUAL CHURCH STEEPLE

In him the whole building is joined together and rises to become a holy temple in the Lord. And in him you too are being built together to become a dwelling in which God lives by his Spirit.

—Ephesians 2:21-22 NIV

The world's most unusual church steeple is located in Port Gibson, Mississippi. I first read about it over fifty years ago in *Ripley's Believe It or Not*. One day Sylvia and I were driving through Mississippi and decided to take a detour from our planned itinerary to visit Port Gibson to see whether or not it was true. Believe it or not, it is true. It is the world's most unusual church steeple and I have a picture to prove it. This church steeple is unusual because instead of the usual cross atop it, this steeple has a fourteen foot replica of a man's right hand with a six foot index finger pointing to the sky! Naturally, there is a story behind it.

It seems that hand was the favorite pulpit gesture of the pastor who led the congregation in the program to erect the building. Unfortunately, the pastor died before the building was finished. The congregation, wishing to honor the pastor, chose this symbol to memorialize him. The symbol reminds us that whatever else a Christian is or is not, he or she should be a hand that points the way to heaven.

"In Him the whole building is joined together and rises to become a holy temple in the Lord. And in Him you too are being built together to become a dwelling in which God lives by His Spirit" (Eph. 2:21-22 NIV).

ALL THE COLORS OF THE RAINBOW

At once I was in the Spirit, and there before me was a throne in heaven with someone sitting on it. And the one who sat there had the appearance of jasper and carnelian. A rainbow, resembling an emerald, encircled the throne.

—Revelation 4:2-3 NIV

When I was a senior in high school during World War II, the United States Navy launched a program which was known as V-12. Young men who were selected for the program were sent to college to train to become engineers or doctors. On the basis of my qualifying test I was selected for the program.

All I had to do was pass the physical. Since I had competed in cross-country and track for three years, I thought that would be a snap. I took a bus to Des Moines for the exam. In typical military fashion we went through an assembly line medical—a series of stations, each one dealing with a different test.

First came hearing. No problem. Then the eye exam—OK. At the third station, I was shown a series of cards with dots on them and asked to identify a number formed by the dots. I learned for the first time in my life that I was color blind! That eliminated me from the program. I remember asking to take the rest of the test. I thought that if I could pass nine out of ten tests that the Navy would still take me, but it didn't work that way. One strike and you're out.

Since I was the first boy from our high school to be selected there was a lot of interest. I remember taking a lot of friendly kidding about being a senior in high school and still not knowing my colors.

One day it suddenly occurred to me that I have never seen a rainbow, at least not the way that other people do. I hope someday to see a rainbow. In the book of Revelation, John writes, "...there before

me was a throne in heaven with someone sitting on it...a rainbow...
surrounded the throne" (Rev. 4:2-3).

My heart leaps up when I behold
A rainbow in the sky.
So was it when my life began,
So is it now I am a man.
So be it when I grow old
Or let me die.

(William Wordsworth)

SEMPER FIDELIS

Be faithful even to the point of death, and I will give you the crown of life.

—Revelation 2:10c NIV

In *Pilgrim's Progress*, that immortal classic of world literature, the author, John Bunyan, depicts a character called Faithful who walks with Christian on his journey to the Celestial City. This is a well-chosen metaphor, for the word "faithful" occurs throughout the Bible.

We are told in the Scriptures that God is faithful. In his first letter to the Corinthians the apostle Paul writes, "God is faithful, by whom you were called into the fellowship of His Son, Jesus Christ our Lord" (1 Cor. 1:9 NKJV).

Three times in the book of Revelation our Lord Jesus Christ is called "the faithful witness." That last book of the Bible begins with this greeting: "Grace to you and peace from Him who is and who was and who is to come,…and from Jesus Christ, the faithful witness, the firstborn of the dead, and the ruler of kings of the earth" (Rev. 1:4-5 NASB).

Those who have preceded us in our walk with God are said to be faithful. In the New Testament we read of "faithful Abraham"; of Moses "who was faithful"; of Lydia "who was judged to be faithful to the Lord"; of Timothy, "faithful in the Lord"; of Tychicus, "a faithful minister in the Lord"; of Onesimus, "a faithful brother"; and of Silvanus, "a faithful brother."

As a matter of fact, the Bible uses the word "faithful" as a name for the true Christian. The apostle Paul addresses his letter to the Ephesians, "Paul, an apostle of Jesus Christ by the will of God, to the saints which are at Ephesus and to the faithful in Christ Jesus" (1:1).

And thus the significance of these words, "Be faithful even to the point of death, and I will give you the crown of life" (Rev. 2:10 NIV).

The motto of every Christian, you see, should be that of the United States Marine Corps: "Semper Fidelis"—always faithful. For, says the Scripture, "it is required of a servant that he be found faithful" (1 Cor. 4:2).

LOOSENED TONGUES

My tongue will speak of Your righteousness and of Your praises all day long.

—Psalm 35:28 NIV

On one occasion Jesus was sitting on a hilltop beside the Sea of Galilee where people brought their sick to be healed. Matthew mentions the mute (among others). Of these Matthew writes, "The people were amazed when they saw the mute speaking" (Matt. 15:30-31 NIV).

Gertrude was a resident in a nursing home. She had not spoken for many months and the staff assumed that she had lost the power of speech. One Sunday afternoon a group of children came to the home to sing for the residents. They sang "Jesus Loves Me":

Jesus loves me, this I know,
For the Bible tells me so.
Little ones to him belong.
They are weak but He is strong.

When they came to the chorus Gertrude sang with them!

Yes, Jesus loves me; Yes, Jesus loves me,
Yes, Jesus loves me; The Bible tells me so. (Anna B. Warner)

No one knows how or why Gertrude regained the power of speech. We only know that Jesus did it.

Jesus loves me, this I know,
Though my hair is white as snow.
Though my sight is growing dim,
Still He bids me trust in Him.

Though my steps are, oh, so slow,
With my hand in His I'll go,
On through life, let come what may,
He'll be there to lead the way. (Unknown)

MY BEST CHRISTMAS GIFT

Thanks be unto God for His indescribable gift!
—2 Corinthians 9:15 NIV

It was December 25, 1944. Our infantry company was in an outpost position to intercept a German counterattack: Operation Nordwind, "the left hook of the Battle of the Bulge." I was keeping busy by chipping away at the frozen ground, trying to enlarge my foxhole and keeping a watchful eye on the hill opposite for any enemy that might appear.

It was a bright, clear day but bitterly cold. Like every other combat infantryman on the western front I had on two sets of wool underwear, two wool uniforms, fatigues, and an army field jacket. I was still as cold as I had ever been in my life. Sometime that afternoon our company commander, Bill Garden, called me over to a little shed near where I was digging my foxhole. As I entered the shed he handed me a package containing a fur lined parka and a pair of waterproof combat boots—a gift from Uncle Sam. I have received many more expensive gifts and many with greater sentimental value, but never have I ever received a gift that was more appreciated.

Now there is something very curious about all this. On Christmas Eve I had slept in a foxhole that had been occupied by a German soldier the night before. He had evidently left in a hurry because he had left his belt. His belt buckle contained the words "Gott mit uns." That means, of course, "God with us." That is the equivalent of the Hebrew "Emmanuel," a title given by the angel to Jesus before His birth. Furthermore, our commander, Bill Garden, was Jewish and the place where he gave me this package was a stable. And, would you believe it, there was a shepherd tending his sheep in a field nearby. I have thought about this strange sequence of events for many years and am always reminded of my best Christmas gift—my Lord and Savior Jesus Christ. "Thanks be unto God for his indescribable gift."

THE TWO-FACED GOD

Jesus Christ is the same yesterday and today and forever.
—Hebrews 13:8

The month of January is named for Janus, the Roman god of beginnings and endings. Janus was represented in art with two faces looking in opposite directions, symbolizing his knowledge of the past and the future. As a matter of fact, the God of Christians is the God of beginnings and endings. In his vision on the Isle of Patmos described in the book of Revelation, the apostle John depicts the risen and ascended Christ in the midst of the churches saying, "I am Alpha and Omega, the beginning and the ending, that which was and is and is to come, the Almighty" (Rev. 1:8).

We often say, "The future is in God's hands." We need also to remember that the past is in God's hands as well. As we look back upon our lives, we can say with Ezra who led the captive Jews from Babylon through the desert to the land of Israel, "The good hand of our God was upon us" (Ezra 8:31b). He is, indeed, the God from whom all blessings flow.

Most of us, as we do an end-of -the-year review of our personal lives, are conscious of the many things that we have done that we ought not to have done and the many things that we have not done that we ought to have done. How thankful we should be that we have a God who "Remembers not our past sins" (Psalm 25:7). "As far as the east is from the west, so far has the Lord removed our sins from us" (Psalm 103:12).

And what does the future hold? No one knows. That is why Paul wrote, "We walk by faith and not by sight" (2 Cor. 5:7). As a popular Christian song has it, "I know not what the future holds, but I know who holds the future." That is what Longfellow said so well:

REFLECTIONS OF A SOLDIER AND SERVANT

I know not what the future hath of marvel or surprise;
Assured alone that life and death his mercy underlies.
I know not where the islands lift their fronded palms in air;
I only know I cannot drift beyond His love and care.

REFLECTING THE SON

It is no longer I who live, but Christ who lives in me.
—Galatians 2:20b RSV

On one occasion an old fisherman was asked by a skeptic, "How do you know that Christ is risen?" The old man replied, "Sometimes when I am out on the sea in my boat I can tell that the sun is risen because I can see its rays reflected in the cloud even before the sun is above the horizon." Then he said, "I know that Christ is risen because I see Him reflected in the lives of my Christian friends."

Dr. Clarence MaCartney, late pastor of the First Presbyterian Church of Philadelphia, said in a sermon on the life of St. Paul, "Paul is the greatest proof of the resurrection of Jesus Christ." The change in Paul's life brought about by his encounter with the risen Savior on the Damascus Road was so profound that no other explanation is possible other than that Paul actually met the risen Christ. Paul went down that road intent on arresting the Christians in Damascus. He came back a missionary of Jesus Christ. He spent the rest of his life reflecting the Son. As he said, "I live, yet not I, but Christ liveth in me" (Rom. 2:20b).

I once heard a minister begin his sermon on Easter Sunday by saying, "Christ is risen. I don't believe it." Then he referred to Paul's words to the Colossians, "Since you have been raised with Christ, seek those things which are above" (3:1). He concluded that if the best evidence of the resurrection of Christ is the lives of today's Christians, then the argument for the resurrection is very weak indeed. What an indictment!

Do you, as a Christian, reflect the Son in your life? Has your life been so changed by your experience of Christ that it is evidence that He rose from the dead?

He lives! He lives! Christ Jesus lives today!
He walks with me and talks with me along life's narrow way.
He lives! He lives! Salvation to impart.
You ask me how I know He lives? He lives within my heart.

(Alfred H. Ackley, "He Lives")

WHY PRAY?

Pray without ceasing. In every thing give thanks: for this is the will of God in Christ Jesus concerning you.

—1 Thessalonians 5:17-18

A father spanked his little boy and sent him off to bed without dessert. As the boy was going up the steps, the father decided that as a deacon in the church he should say something spiritual. "I'm going to pray for you," he called out.

The boy replied, "You can if you want to, but it won't do any good."

That young man was not the first to express such an opinion in my presence. I was in a discussion group when one of the ladies said, "It doesn't make any difference whether or not we pray. God does what He wants to do anyway."

Gandhi came to the opposite conclusion based on his knowledge of God. He said, "Because I believe in God, I believe in prayer."

The lady had a point, however. God does what He wants to do. One of the things that He wants to do is answer prayer! Jesus put it this way: "If you then, though you are evil, know how to give good gifts to your children, how much more will your Father in heaven give the Holy Spirit to those who ask Him!" (Luke 11:13 NIV). In that same passage He made this wonderful promise: "Ask and it shall be given you; seek and you shall find; knock and it shall be opened unto you" (11:9). The truth of the matter is that God is far more willing to answer our prayers than we are to offer them. It was Archbishop Trench who said, "Prayer is not overcoming God's reluctance; it is laying hold of his highest willingness."

"Let us then approach the throne of grace with confidence, so that we may receive mercy and find grace to help us in our time of need" (Heb. 4:16 NIV).

HIS APPOINTED PLACE

For to you it has been granted on behalf of Christ, not only to believe in Him, but also to suffer for His sake, having the same conflict which you saw in me and now hear is in me.

—Philippians 1:29-30 NKJV

In Genesis 12:10 we read of Abraham's entrance into the Promised Land: "Now there was a famine in the land. So Abraham went down to Egypt to sojourn there." These words do not speak of the doubt, disappointment, and disillusionment that Abraham must have experienced at this time. He had left his ancestral home in Ur of the Chaldees and made the long and difficult journey to the land that God had promised to him and his descendants. But when he arrived, there was a famine in the land. Some promise! Some land!

One day when we were serving a church in Michigan a lady came into my office and said, "I have a question about your sermons."

I told her, "You're lucky. Most people have a lot of questions about my sermons."

She continued, "Well, what I don't understand is why you are always talking about this disappointed place." Well, if you have ever been in Northern Michigan in the winter you can understand why someone might talk about "this disappointed place."

But I knew that was something that I had never said. In fact, I had to think for awhile to come up with something which I had said which might be mistaken for "this disappointed place." When I did I had to laugh as I told this dear lady, "I'm not saying 'this disappointed place.' I'm saying, 'His appointed place.'"

And that was Abraham's problem. He had mistaken God's appointed place for this disappointed place. It is a problem that we all have at times, because many times God's blessings come to us in disguise. But this experience of Abraham teaches us that it is possible to turn this disappointed place into His appointed place. When Abraham at last arrived in the land of promise the Lord appeared to him and said, "To your descendants I will give this land." And then we read, "So he built an altar to the Lord." So, to turn this disappointed place into His appointed place review the promises of God and build an altar there.

"Many are the afflictions of the righteous, but the Lord delivers him out of them all" (Psalm 34:19).

"In the world you shall have tribulation, but be of good cheer, I have overcome the world" (John 16:33).

"It is given us in behalf of Christ, not only to believe on Him, but also to suffer for His sake" but "the sufferings of this present time are not worthy to be compared with the glory that shall be revealed in us" (Phil. 1:29).

STRENGTH THROUGH WEAKNESS

And He [Jesus] said unto me, "My grace is sufficient for thee: for my strength is made perfect in weakness." Most gladly therefore will I rather glory in my infirmities, that the power of Christ may rest upon me.
—2 Corinthians 12:9

I was thirteen years old at the time. I was throwing a football back and forth with a friend when I fell over backwards and broke my left arm. My dad took me to St. Luke's Hospital emergency room where our family physician, Dr. Hess, met us and set the arm. One of the things that I learned from that experience is that the callus that forms where a bone has been broken and reset is stronger than the bone itself.

There is a principle there that applies to much of life. God says in His Word, "My strength is made perfect in weakness" (2 Cor. 12:9).

There is no better example of that principle than the man who wrote those words. In his second letter to the Corinthians, Paul speaks of his brokenness: "Five times I received from the Jews the forty lashes minus one. Three times I was beaten with rods, once I was stoned, three times I was shipwrecked....I have labored and toiled and have often gone without sleep; I have known hunger and thirst and gone without food; I have been cold and naked" (2 Cor. 11:24-27 NIV).

In addition to these things Paul suffered an incurable affliction which he called his "thorn in the flesh." He prayed three times that God would relieve him of this affliction but instead God said, "My grace is sufficient for thee; for my strength is made perfect in weakness." It is only when we recognize and admit our weakness that we receive the strength of God. Human extremity is God's opportunity.

A little boy was trying to move a large rock in the yard of his home, but without success. His father asked him, "Are you using all your strength?"

Somewhat exasperated by the question the boy answered, "Of course I am."

The father replied, "No, you aren't. You haven't asked me to help."

Remember, "When I am weak, then I am strong" (2 Cor. 12:10).

SPIRITUAL PRIDE

A man's pride brings him low, but a man of lowly spirit gains honor.
—Proverbs 29:23 NIV

I once saw a cartoon about pride in a Christian magazine. The various frames depicted pride of face, pride of race, pride of place, and the last frame read, "Worst of all—pride of grace."

Spiritual pride can take many forms: the size of our congregations, the beauty of our house of worship, our doctrine, our spiritual gifts, and other such prideful things. One lady was asked to explain to a friend the difference between her denomination and another denomination with a similar name. The lady replied, "We're just like them only better." A man was asked to explain the difference between certain religious groups. He explained that this group is noted for its emphasis on education and that one on social activism. "But," he said, "when it comes to humility, we're tops!" Hopefully these people were both joking, but there is sometimes real truth in humor. We may all well pray with the one who asked, "Lord, make me humble but don't let me know it."

However, there is a spiritual pride that is justified. The apostle Paul put it this way: "May I never boast except in the cross of our Lord Jesus Christ, through which the world has been crucified to me, and I to the world" (Gal. 6:14 NIV).

In Romans 1:16 Paul writes, "I am not ashamed of the gospel, because it is the power of God for the salvation of everyone who believes" (NIV). One Chicago church erected a beautiful sign on its front lawn that read, "Proud of the Gospel."

SPEAKING THE TRUTH IN LOVE

Speaking the truth in love, we will in all things grow up into Him who is the Head, that is, Christ.

—Ephesians 4:15 NIV

On one occasion a lady invited one of her friends to attend church with her to hear her new minister. On the drive back home the visitor asked her friend, "Why did the church let the last minister go?"

The lady replied, "Oh, he was always telling people that if they didn't repent of their sins that they would all go to hell."

"I don't understand," replied the friend. "That's what the new minister said this morning."

The lady answered, "I know, but the other one acted like he enjoyed it."

It is true, you know: it's not only what you say but how you say it. The apostle Paul admonished the Christians at Ephesus to speak the truth in love (see Ephesians 4:15). Recently, a United States senator who had served many years in the Senate announced that he would not seek re-election. His reason for not running again was the fact that the debate in Congress was filled with such rancor and bitterness that it was no longer possible for the Senate to make decisions in the interest of the common good.

Of course, the church has not been exempt from such charges of strife and clamor. Sadly, many theological debates have ended with one of the parties being burned at the stake.

How different from the teaching of our Lord and His apostles. Our Lord Jesus Christ, the personification of both love and truth, said, "Love your enemies, do good to them which hate you, bless them that curse you, and pray for them which despitefully use you" (Luke 6:27-28). The letters of the apostle Paul written from his prison cell evidence love and compassion for those who put him there.

Faith of our fathers! We will love both friend and foe in all our strife;
And preach Thee, too, as love knows how, by kindly word and virtuous life.

(Frederick W. Fabor, "Faith of Our Fathers")

THE CHIEF SHEPHERD

And when the Chief Shepherd appears you will receive the crown of glory that will never fade away.

—1 Peter 5:4 NIV

A man who was pressed by a friend to explain his faith simply recited the Twenty-third Psalm. When he had finished he said, "That is my creed. I need, I desire no other. I learned it from my mother's lips. I have repeated it every morning for the last twenty years. Yet I do not half understand it; I am only now beginning to spell out its infinite meaning, and death will come on me with the task unfinished. But, by the grace of Jesus, I will hold on by this Psalm as my creed, and will strive to believe it and to live for it; for I know that it will lead me to the cross; it will guide me to glory."

Christians who read this Psalm see Jesus as the shepherd in it. For in the New Testament Jesus is often spoken of as a shepherd. In John's Gospel Jesus says, "I am the Good Shepherd; the Good Shepherd gives his life for the sheep" (John 10:11). The writer of the epistle to the Hebrews says, "Now the God of peace who brought again from the dead our Lord Jesus, that Great Shepherd of the sheep through the blood of the everlasting covenant make you perfect in every good work to do His will, working in you that which is well pleasing in His sight" (Heb. 13:20-21). And Peter speaks of Jesus when he declares, "When the Chief Shepherd appears you will receive the crown of glory that will never fade away" (1 Peter 5:4).

The one who follows Jesus finds all of his needs met in Him. I shall not want rest, for He makes me to lie down. I shall not want refreshment, for He makes me to lie down in green pastures. I shall not want salvation, for He restores my soul. I shall not want guidance, for He leads me in the paths of righteousness. I shall not want companionship, for You are with me. I shall not want comfort, for Your rod and staff comfort me. I shall not want joy, for You anoint my head with oil. I shall not want anything, for my cup runs over. I shall not want anything in this life, for surely goodness and mercy shall follow me all the days of my life. I shall not want anything in eternity, for I shall dwell in the house of the Lord forever.

EVERY TONGUE CONFESS

Every tongue should confess that Jesus Christ is Lord, to the glory of God the Father.

—Philippians 2:11 NKJV

Ed went to the office of his plant superintendent to register a complaint. He was met by the second in charge who inquired as to the nature of his complaint. Ed replied that he would explain it to the superintendent. The number-two man explained that it was necessary to follow the chain of command. To reinforce his statement, he pointed to the door of the super's office and said, "If Jesus Christ goes through that door he has to see me first."

Why Jesus Christ? Why not the President of the United States or Secretary General of the United Nations or the Queen? Why Jesus Christ? Because even unbelievers recognize the supremacy of Jesus Christ. The apostle Paul foresaw a day when every tongue will confess that Jesus Christ is Lord (see Philippians 2:11).

To be a Christian is to acknowledge the Lordship of Jesus Christ by life and lips. In the epistle to the Romans Paul writes, "If you confess with your mouth, 'Jesus is Lord,' and believe in your heart God raised him from the dead, you will be saved" (Rom. 10:9 NIV). Queen Victoria once said, "If Jesus Christ should return to earth today, I would lay the crowns of the British Empire at His feet."

> Holy God, we praise Thy name;
> Lord of all, we bow before Thee;
> All on earth Thy scepter claim,
> All in heav'n above adore Thee;
> Infinite Thy vast domain,
> Everlasting is Thy reign.
> (Te Deum, c. 4th century, trans. Clarence Walworth)

SPIRITUAL REST

Come to me, all you who are weary and burdened, and I will give you rest. Take my yoke upon you and learn from me, for I am gentle and humble in heart, and you will find rest for your souls. For my yoke is easy and my burden is light.

—Matthew 11:28-30 NIV

I was making my first "get acquainted" pastoral call in my new congregation one weekday afternoon. I was visiting Annie, a deaconess and Sunday school teacher. In the middle of our conversation she blurted out, "Pastor, my husband's a drunkard." Most wives would say, "My husband is an alcoholic" or "My husband has a drinking problem." In Annie's case, "drunkard" was the right word.

Many Sunday mornings she would come to breakfast to find her husband unconscious on the kitchen floor. She would clean up the blood and vomit, drag her husband up to bed, and walk six blocks to church to teach her Sunday school class of junior girls about the love of Jesus. As I learned more of Annie's situation, I wondered how anyone could live like that and still be the sweet, kind, and gentle person that she was.

Then one day I learned the answer. In our monthly newsletter there was a feature called "Member of the Month." I would interview some person from the congregation and write an article for the newsletter. One of the standard questions was "What is your favorite Bible verse?" Most people had trouble answering that one. But not Annie.

When I asked that question, Annie's voice brightened as she said, "Oh, Pastor, my favorite verse is Matthew 11:28." Then she quoted it, "Come unto me all you that labor and are heavy laden. I will give you rest; take my yoke upon you and learn of me for I am meek and lowly in heart and you shall find rest for your soul."

I could never explain to anyone how those words on the printed page could so affect a human life, but I saw it with my own eyes.

> I heard the voice of Jesus say,
> "Come unto me and rest;
> Lay down, thou weary one, lay down
> Thy head upon my breast."
> I came to Jesus as I was,
> Weary, and worn and sad;
> I found in Him a resting place,
> And He has made me glad.
>
> (Horatius Bonar, "I Heard the Voice of Jesus Say")

THE POWER OF THE BLOOD

*But if we walk in the light, as He is in the light, we have fellowship with
one another, and the blood of Jesus, His Son, purifies us from all sin.*
—1 John 1:7 NIV

I was just about to receive my thirty-sixth blood transfusion. I had
been to the clinic so many times that all the nurses knew me by name.
Nevertheless, they asked all the usual questions, including my name,
before beginning the procedure. I thought I would insert a little humor
into the situation, so when I was asked my name, I replied, "I used to
be Dean Nemecek, but after thirty-six units of blood I am not sure
who I am." The nurses laughed even though they had probably heard
some variation of that joke a hundred times. Later as I had time to
reflect on this incident I was reminded of something to which I had
previously given only intellectual assent, that is, that I owed my life to
those thirty-six people.

In my reverie my thoughts went back to the day that I was ordained to the ministry. In the service that evening the male chorus of
the church sang an old gospel song, "The Blood Will Never Lose It's
Power." I was seeing that truth confirmed in my body. It is true of my
soul as well. "The blood of Jesus Christ, God's Son, cleanses us from all
sin" (1 John 1:7).

What can wash away my sin?
Nothing but the blood of Jesus.
What can make me whole again?
Nothing but the blood of Jesus.
(Robert Lowry, "Nothing But the Blood")

GRANT US OUR PETTINESS

Be anxious for nothing, but in everything by prayer and supplication, with thanksgiving, let your requests be made known to God; and the peace of God, which surpasses all understanding, will guard your hearts and minds through Christ Jesus.

—Philippians 4:6-7 NKJV

The minister had written out his pastoral prayer so as to avoid any of those pulpit blunders which seem to be so prevalent. The written prayer ended, "Grant us our petitions, O Lord." Instead the pastor read, "Grant us our pettiness, O Lord." The sad thing is that no one seemed to notice!

Perhaps the pastor's spoken word was nearer the truth than his written one. As J. B. Phillips put it, "Your prayers are too small." We are like little children playing at the water's edge while the great ocean of God's promises lie unexplored before us. There are no limits to the extent of God's love. "In *everything* by prayer and supplication with thanksgiving let your requests be made known unto God" (Phil. 4:5), and "My God shall supply *all* your needs according to His riches in glory by Christ Jesus" (4:19). When we pray we should remember that we come at God's invitation. "Let us therefore come boldly unto the throne of grace that we may obtain grace and mercy to help in time of need" (Heb. 4:16). Archbishop Trench has reminded us, "Prayer is not overcoming God's reluctance; it is laying hold of his highest willingness."

Thou are coming to a King
Large petitions with thee bring.

To help us avoid pettiness in our prayers we should always offer the prayer that never fails, "Not my will, but Thine be done" (Luke 22:42).

71

It is the prayer that Jesus offered in the Garden of Gethsemane as He contemplated the cross. It is what He taught us in the Lord's Prayer, "Thy will be done on earth as it is in heaven" (Matt. 6:10b). That translates, "Thy will be done in me as it is in heaven."

D. L. Moody went shopping for a new doll with his little daughter. After she had made her selection and they were leaving the store, Mr. Moody said to her, "I'm surprised that you picked that one. I was going to buy you a much bigger one."

After that whenever they went shopping to buy something for her, his little daughter would say, "You choose, Papa. You choose." Yes, it's true God always gives His best to those who leave the choice with Him.

GA-GA AND MOO-MOO

And Jesus grew in wisdom and stature, and in favor with God and men.

—Luke 2:52 NIV

I suppose it's harmless enough—baby talk, that is—particularly, adults talking baby talk to their children or grandchildren. However, I must admit that I still find it disconcerting to hear a sixty-year-old grandfather refer to himself as Ga-Ga and his wife as Moo-Moo when talking to his grandchildren. I am still not sure why adults talk baby talk to their children and grandchildren. Perhaps it enables the adult to communicate with the child better by speaking his or her language. Perhaps it enables the adult to better "bond" with the child.

Pediatricians and psychologists seem to be divided over the question of the relative value of using baby talk with children. My own family seems to be divided on the issue. Some of my grandchildren called me "Papa" until they reached a certain stage when they referred to me as granddad or grandpa. Others were taught to call me "Granddad" or "Grandfather" from the very beginning. I have to admit that one of my fondest memories from the time when the grandchildren were small was of our oldest grandchild, Sean, crawling over the threshold of our home calling "Papa, Papa." On the other hand, Sean's son, Benjamin, doesn't seem to have any problem with the concept of "great-grandfather."

Luke, the beloved physician, is the only one of the four gospel authors to make any reference to the childhood of Jesus: "The child grew in wisdom and stature and in favor with God and man" (Luke 1:80). The truth of the matter is that God has his own time table for each child. In a book entitled *Stories I Couldn't Tell When I Was a Pastor,* Bruce McIver tells of his concern for his three-year-old daughter who had never spoken a complete sentence. Rev. McIver was attempting to give a pill to the family dog. The dog kept spitting the pill out. It was then that the three-year-old spoke her first sentence—"Take the pill, you damn dog!" Jesus said, "Let the little children come to me, and do not hinder them, for the kingdom of heaven belongs to such as these" (Matt. 19:14 NIV). "Unless you change and become like little children, you will never enter the kingdom of heaven" (Matt. 18:3 NIV).

KRAMER AND ME

Then he calls his friends and neighbors together and says, "Rejoice with me; I have found my lost sheep."

—Luke 15:6 NIV

I have been reading *Marley and Me*, the number-one non-fiction best seller in the United States. The book is about a young couple in Florida and their dog, Marley, a yellow Labrador Retriever. The book brought back memories of two other yellow Labs I had known: Mandy and Kramer. Mandy belonged to my sister and her late husband, Don Stastny. Mandy was not only the family pet but was also Don's duck hunting companion, an activity which Mandy loved and excelled at. The other yellow Lab was Kramer, owned by my daughter, Beth.

I knew Kramer the better of the two because occasionally Grandma Sylvia and I would "sit" with Jessica and Mike, Beth's children. That involved taking care of Kramer, as well as a cat, a gerbil, a talking parrot, and a boa constrictor. Kramer was very gentle, good with the children, and actually considered himself part of the family. When people came to the house Kramer thought that they came to see him and greeted them accordingly with sloppy kisses.

Kramer loved the out-of-doors. His ventures outdoors were usually a daily walk on a leash. You had to be careful not to use the word "walk" in Kramer's hearing. Otherwise he would bring you his leash expecting you to take him for a walk. Because he loved the outdoors so much, Kramer would try to get outside any way he could. I learned that lesson the hard way.

I was going out the back door to get some firewood when Kramer shot by me and was loose. Although Jessica assured me that he would come back, I didn't want to chance it so got in the car to drive through the village hoping to find him. I didn't want to tell my daughter that I'd lost her dog. At least it wasn't the boa constrictor!

75

I didn't have any trouble finding Kramer. He had a two-square-block area that he toured. As he went by, the other dogs who saw him barked and I could see or hear the route that he was following. I finally caught up with him and opened the passenger-side door and called to him. He came over and put his front paws in the car. I patted the passenger-side seat hoping that he would get in. He just looked at me as if to say, "How dumb do you think I am?" Then he took off again.

Jessica was right. About a half hour later I saw Kramer in the back-yard playing in the foot of snow that had covered the ground. I went into the yard and called him. He came within about eight feet of me and then turned away. We played this game for awhile. Then I noticed that Kramer would bury his head in the snow, covering his eyes and ears. Then he would throw his head back tossing the snow up in the air. Each time that he did this I moved a little closer to him until finally I was able to grab his collar. He never resisted or tried to pull away but simply walked obediently beside me as I led him back into the house. He seemed to be saying, "Well, it was fun while it lasted."

Kramer's undoing was due to the fact that he buried his head in the snow. I think he assumed that since he couldn't see me that I couldn't see him. There are a great many people who go through life like those in *The Blind Men and the Elephant,* each assuming that his view is the correct one and the only one.

> Open my eyes that I may see
> Glimpses of truth Thou hast for me;
> Place in my hands the wonderful key
> That shall unclasp and set me free.
> (Clara H. Scott, "Open My Eyes, That I May See")

DO YOU HAVE ANY HOPE?

Happy is he who has the God of Jacob for his help, whose hope is in the LORD his God.

—Psalm 146:5 NKJV

In 1954 when Dr. Billy Graham was conducting his first Greater London Crusade, he was granted an interview with Prime Minister Winston Churchill. As the evangelist was ushered into Mr. Churchill's office at No. 10 Downing Street the great statesman looked up from his desk with a scowl on his face and asked, "Young man, do you have any hope?" Dr. Graham says that he then sat down with the Prime Minister and read to him several passages from the New Testament containing the message of Christian hope.

The Prime Minister's question seems somewhat out of character for him. For this man, with his smile and V for victory sign, was the very symbol of hope for millions of people during the dark days of World War II. This is the same man who once said, "I am an optimist. It does not seem much use to be anything else."

On the other hand, Mr. Churchill had adequate reason for pessimism. Britain was in the midst of a deep economic depression. Her empire was disintegrating. The Cold War was in its deepest freeze and the possibility of a nuclear holocaust loomed on the horizon.

The Scripture says that every Christian should "be ready to give an answer to everyone that asks a reason for the hope that is within us" (1 Peter 3:15). What is the reason for our hope? It is the gospel of Jesus Christ. The Bible speaks of the hope of the everlasting gospel and reminds us that "If in this life only we have hope in Christ, we are of all men most miserable" (1 Cor. 15:19).

And what is the gospel? In 1 Corinthians 15 Paul defines the gospel: "Christ died for our sins according to the Scriptures; and that he was buried, and that he rose again the third day, according to the

Scriptures" (vv. 3-4). It is this message, the good news that Christ died for our sins and rose again, that is the basis of the Christian's hope in every circumstance of life.

> My hope is in the Lord, who gave himself for me,
> And paid the price of all my sin at Calvary.
> For me he died; for me he lives,
> And everlasting life and light he freely gives.
> (Norman J. Clayton, "My Hope Is in the Lord")

TRUST AND OBEY

Train up a child in the way he should go: and when he is old, he will not depart from it.

—Proverbs 22:6

Great-grandson Benjamin, age 4, is learning to spell. His parents, Sean and Amy, can no longer talk about having p-i-z-z-a for dinner. Ben's translation is not always completely accurate. Amy was in the process of disciplining him and asked, "Do you know what o-b-e-y means?"

"Yes," said Benjamin. "Spank!" At least he was in the ballpark.

In commenting on the words of Jesus, "Whoever does not receive the kingdom of God as a little child shall not enter into it," William Barclay in *The Daily Study Bible* points out the childlike characteristics that Jesus is talking about. "Children are naturally *obedient*." "Their instinct is to obey," he writes. In his letter to the Ephesians, the apostle Paul gives instruction on child discipline. "Fathers, don't overcorrect your children,…Bring them up with Christian teaching in Christian discipline" (Eph. 6:4 Phillips). A review of thirty years of research on child discipline in the home and in the classroom indicated that two words can summarize the best attitude of parent or teacher when disciplining the child—*firm* and *friendly*. That is exactly what Paul says in the Ephesians passage.

The other childlike qualities that open the doors to the kingdom, according to Barclay, in addition to obedience are **wonder** and **trust**. It is worth noting what else Barclay says about the *obedience* of children: "In their heart of hearts their parents' word is law. So should it be with us and God."

When we walk with the Lord
In the light of His Word
What a glory He sheds on our way!
While we do His good will
He abides with us still,
And with all who will trust and obey.

(John H. Sammis, "Trust and Obey")

THE PREACHING OF THE CROSS

The preaching of the cross is to them that perish foolishness, but unto us which are saved it is the power of God.

—1 Corinthians 1:18

There is something very strange about this text. It would seem that Paul's reasoning is in error. For he contrasts foolishness with power. It would seem more logical to contrast foolishness with wisdom or weakness with power. Thus, we might think that Paul would have said, "The preaching of the cross is to them that perish foolishness, but unto us which are saved it is the wisdom of God" or "The preaching of the cross is to them that perish weakness but unto us which are saved it is the power of God."

In any case, we know that the preaching of the cross is both the wisdom and the power of God to those who are saved. As a matter of fact, in the context of this verse Paul speaks of Christ as the wisdom of God and the power of God. And of course one may not understand the person of Christ apart from the cross of Christ.

Thus, the cross is the wisdom of God to those who believe. It is the essential doctrine of our Christian faith. No one who reads the Bible can fail to notice the importance of the cross in the plan of redemption outlined in the Bible. Even the Old Testament, written centuries before Jesus was born in Bethlehem, speaks of His cross. The prophet Isaiah, who lived some 700 years before Jesus, wrote, "He was wounded for our transgressions; He was bruised for our iniquities; the chastisement of our peace was upon Him and with His stripes we are healed" (Isaiah 53:5). Those words are quoted several times in the New Testament as referring to the death of our Lord Jesus Christ.

In the preaching of Jesus and the apostles the message of the cross is central. If we want to know the significance of the life and ministry of our Lord we ought to ask Him. He answered that question for us when He said, "The Son of Man came not to be ministered unto, but to minister and give His life a ransom for many" (Matt. 20:28). The apostle John said of the cross, "Herein is love, not that we loved God, but that He loved us and sent His Son to be the sacrifice for our sins" (1 John 4:10). Peter spoke of the cross of Christ: "Who in His own body bore our sins on the tree that we being dead to sin might live unto godliness by whose stripes we are healed" (1 Peter 2:24). And Paul wrote, "God shows His love toward us in that while we were yet sinners Christ died for us" (Rom. 5:8). That is the message of the Christian faith—the message of the cross.

THE CHURCH OF THE RESURRECTION

Then the disciples went out and preached everywhere, and the Lord worked with them and confirmed His word by the signs that accompanied it.

—Mark 16:20 NIV

Dr. Robert Speer, the great missionary statesman, wrote this in one of his many books about our Lord Jesus Christ: "There is a kingdom of Christ that bears witness to the fact that something lifted it out of death when He hung on the cross. It was saved by nothing less than His rising again from the dead." So it is that the church of Jesus Christ today is the church of the resurrection—the church that received life when He rose from the dead.

We see evidence of that miraculous transformation in Mark 16. There can be no doubt that the death of Christ left the church in defeat, doubt, and despair. The women came to the tomb to embalm a dead body—not to worship a risen savior. When the angel appeared and announced the resurrection to the women we read, "and they trembled and were amazed; neither said they anything to any man; for they were afraid" (v. 8b).

He first appeared to Mary Magdalene, out of whom he had cast seven devils. When she told the mourning disciples, "they, when they had heard that He was alive, and had been seen of her, believed not" (v. 11). "After that He appeared in another form unto two of them, as they walked, and went into the country. And they went and told it unto the others; neither believed they them" (vv. 12-13). "Afterwards, He appeared unto the eleven as they sat at meat, and upbraided them with their unbelief and hardness of heart, because they believed not them which had seem Him after He was risen " (v. 14).

Gradually, the truth of what really happened dawned upon them and they believed. For in the last verse of this gospel we read, "and they went forth, and preached everywhere, the Lord working with them, and confirming the word with signs following." Something lifted the church out of death when He hung upon the cross. It was saved by nothing less than His rising again from the dead. Yes, we are the church of the resurrection.

DANCING WITH THE DAFFODILS

Consider the lilies, how they grow; they neither toil nor spin; and yet I say to you, even Solomon in all his glory was not arrayed like one of these.
—Luke 12:27 NKJV

When I was in seminary I attended classes in the mornings, worked at Hartford Insurance in the afternoons, and studied in the evenings. Obviously, there was not much to brighten up our lives. So occasionally I would buy Sylvia a bouquet of daffodils on my way home from work.

Daffodils have remained a favorite for nearly sixty years. We have a thousand of them blooming in our backyard even as I write! They are a reminder of God's unfailing provision for us. As Paul put it, "And my God will meet all your needs according to His glorious riches in Christ Jesus" (Phil. 4:19 NIV).

Jesus talked about the lilies of the valley. The "lily" that Jesus was talking about was an anemone or windflower. Certainly daffodils carry the same message. "See how the lilies of the field grow. They do not labor or spin. Yet I tell you that not even Solomon in all his splendor was dressed like one of these. If that is how God clothes the grass of the field, which is here today and tomorrow is thrown into the fire, will He not much more clothe you, O you of little faith?" (Matt. 6:28-30 NIV).

> I wandered lonely as a cloud
> That floats on high o'er vales and hills,
> When all at once I saw a crowd,—
> A host, of golden daffodils,

REFLECTIONS OF A SOLDIER AND SERVANT

Beside the lake, beneath the trees,
Fluttering and dancing in the breeze...

And then my heart with pleasure filled,
And danced with the daffodils.
(from "Daffodils," by William Wordsworth)

BEARING THE CROSS

I have been crucified with Christ; it is no longer I who live, but Christ lives in me; and the life which I now live in the flesh I live by faith in the Son of God, who loved me and gave Himself for me.
—Galatians 2:20 NKJV

Dr. Everett Swanson, the founder of Compassion, a mission to Korean orphans, once told of a chaplain in the South Korean Army who learned on the battlefield what it means to confess Jesus as Lord. He was captured by the North Koreans. He was standing in the street with a group of other prisoners waiting to be taken to a North Korean prison camp when a North Korean officer noticed the cross on his lapel designating him as a chaplain. The officer walked up to the chaplain and ordered him to remove the cross. The chaplain refused.

The officer took his pistol from his holster, cocked it, and pointed it at the chaplain's head and said, "Take off the cross or you die."

The chaplain replied, "The cross stays."

Just at that moment there was shooting outside the village by South Korean soldiers attempting to retake the town. In the confusion that followed the chaplain escaped. Years later he became Chief of Chaplains of the South Korean Army. He had met the supreme test. He had said, "Not my will but Thine be done." He had taken up his cross to follow Jesus. He had confessed him as Lord.

None of us will ever likely be called upon to face a situation like that. On the other hand, to be a Christian means to bear the cross. Jesus said, "If any man will come after me, let him deny himself and take up his cross and follow me" (Matt. 16:24). The apostle Paul described his Christian life in these words: "I am crucified with Christ; nevertheless I live, yet not I but Christ liveth in me; and the life which I now live I live in the flesh I live by the faith of the Son of God who loved me and gave Himself for me" (Gal. 2:20). To bear the cross is to live in the spirit of the prayer that Jesus offered in the Garden of Gethsemane, "Not my will, but Thine be done" (Luke 22:42).

> Jesus, I my cross have taken,
> All to leave and follow Thee;
> Destitute, despised, forsaken,
> Thou from hence my all shall be:
> Perish every fond ambition,
> All I've sought, and hoped and known,
> Yet how rich is my condition,
> God and heaven are still my own!
>
> (Henry F. Lyte, "Jesus, I My Cross Have Taken")

SERMON TO THE BIRDS

Look at the birds of the air; they do not sow or reap or store away in barns, and yet your heavenly Father feeds them. Are you not much more valuable than they?

— Matthew 6:26 NIV

"My little sisters, the birds, much bounden are ye unto God, your Creator, and always in every place ought ye to praise Him, for that He hath given you liberty to fly about everywhere, and hath also given you double and triple raiment; moreover, He preserved your seed in the ark of Noah, that your race might not perish out of the world; still more are ye beholden to Him for the element of the air which he hath appointed for you; beyond all this, ye sow not, neither do you reap; and God feedeth you, and giveth you the streams and fountains for your drink; the mountains and the valleys for your refuge and the high trees whereon to make your nests; and because ye know not how to spin or sew, God clotheth you, you and your children; wherefore your Creator loveth you much, seeing that he hath bestowed on you so many benefits; and therefore, my little sisters, beware of the sin of ingratitude, and study always to give praises unto God." (St. Francis of Assisi)

> Why should I feel discouraged,
> Why should the shadows come,
> Why should my heart be lonely,
> And long for heav'n and home,
> When Jesus is my portion?
> My constant friend is He
> His eye is on the sparrow,
> And I know He watches me.
>
> (Civilla D. Martin, "His Eye Is on the Sparrow")

DO WE NEED THE TEN COMMANDMENTS IN THE TWENTY-FIRST CENTURY?

Whoever therefore breaks one of the least of these commandments, and teaches men so, shall be called least in the kingdom of heaven; but whoever does and teaches them, he shall be called great in the kingdom of heaven.

—Matthew 5:19 NKJV

In the first half of the last century Christian theology was the focus of much controversy. Such doctrines as the biblical account of creation, the inspiration and authority of the Scriptures, the deity of Christ, and the miracles of the Bible came under attack by people outside the church as well as some within the church. Although many people abandoned historic Christian theology, nevertheless, Christian values and Christian morals were accepted and served as the normative standard for our society.

At the present time it is Christian values and morals that are being challenged. Situation ethics and the sexual revolution have led many people to believe that there are no longer any moral absolutes. In the name of freedom this generation resents discipline; it does not like commandments of any kind.

Unlimited freedom and unrestricted permission to experiment are the contemporary demands. In a situation such as this liberty can very easily become license and the right to experiment can become the right to wreck one's own life and the lives of others. As one of our poets wrote:

In vain we call old notions fudge,
And bend our conscience to our dealing;
The Ten Commandments will not budge,
And stealing will continue stealing.

(James Russell Lowell, "Stealing")

91

It is therefore well and good that this generation should be confronted with the uncompromising demand of the Ten Commandments. It may not accept them, but it cannot ignore them.

WHEN THE CIRCUS CAME TO TOWN

So whether you eat or drink or whatever you do, do it all for the glory of God.

—1 Corinthians 10:31 NIV

"Greatest Show on Earth, a Real Traffic-Stopper" Tuesday's headline in Rochester's *Democrat and Chronicle* read. There was even a photo of the elephants from the Ringling Brothers and Barnum and Bailey Circus on their way to the arena. It reminded me of another day when the circus came to town.

Chris, one of our students at Roberts Wesleyan College, got a big job with the circus—a really big job. He walked behind the elephants in the parade—carrying a shovel! The pay was good, but Chris didn't care much for the fringe benefits. What he really didn't like was when he got back to campus, students teased him about being the "super duper pooper scooper!"

Wait a minute, though, before you write Chris off. Can you imagine what the parade would have been without him? The marching band? The tuba player? When Peter Marshall was chaplain of the United States Senate, he was also pastor of the New York Avenue Presbyterian Church in Washington, D.C. He often gave thanks for garbage collectors—one of those people that you never miss until they're not there.

Have you ever thought of the number of people who serve you every week—people that you rarely see? The garbage man, the mailman, the meter men, etc. One thing that always impresses me about the apostle Paul as I read his story in the book of Acts is that he was always the same man, whether he was talking to the slave Onesimus or King Agrippa. He always respected people for the content of their character, not the position they held. He said, "I am become all things to all men that I might win some to Christ."

93

THIS ONE THING I KNOW

This is love: not that we loved God, but that he loved us and sent his Son as an atoning sacrifice for our sins.

—1 John 4:10 NIV

The Swiss theologian Karl Barth was speaking to a conference of theologians. In a question-and-answer period he was asked, "As a result of your many years of study of Christian theology, what would you say was your most important discovery?"

Dr. Barth replied, "Jesus loves me; This I know; For the Bible tells me so."

What does the Bible have to say about the love of Jesus? The apostle Paul wrote, "God shows His love toward us in that while we were still sinners Christ died for us" (Rom. 5:8). John, the beloved disciple, declared, "Herein is love; not that we loved God, but that He loved us and sent His Son to be the sacrifice for our sins" (1 John 4:10).

Yes, more than anything else it is the cross of Christ that reveals God's great love for us. When Billy Graham was on a preaching mission in India, he visited Mother Teresa in her hospice in Calcutta. As she sat holding a dying man, Dr. Graham asked her, "Why do you do this?" Mother Teresa did not answer, she simply pointed to the crucifix on the wall.

I need no other argument;
I need no other plea;
It is enough that Jesus died;
And that He did for me.

Lidie H. Edmunds, "My Faith Has Found a Resting Place"

DOUBLE-TALK

I will take heed to my ways that I sin not with my tongue.

—Psalm 39:1a

"If George Washington were alive today, he would turn over in his grave."

"It was so dark you couldn't see your face in front of you."

"Isn't it pretty? The lake comes right up to the shore."

"I never liked you and I always will."

"Come see us again soon. We miss you almost as much as if you were here."

The above statements are examples of double-talk. The dictionary defines double-talk as "talk or writing that to all appearances is earnest and meaningful but is actually a mixture of sense and unintelligible verbiage and gibberish."

James, the brother of our Lord, speaks of another kind of double-talk in his epistle: "From the same mouth come blessing and cursing" (James 3:10). He points out the great potential of the tongue for good or evil when he compares it to a fire, the rudder of a ship, and the bit in a horse's mouth. As Luther said, "The tongue guides men either to virtue or to vice."

Think of the potential for evil of human speech. Two of the Ten Commandments have to do with sins of speech: "Thou shalt not take the name of the Lord thy God in vain" and "Thou shalt not bear false witness against thy neighbor." In James's short book he mentions five sins of the tongue: blasphemy (2:7), cursing (3:9), boasting (3:5), lying (3:14), and evil speaking (4:11). The only unpardonable sin, blasphemy against the Holy Spirit, is a sin of the tongue.

The potential of human speech for good is even greater. With speech we confess Christ, teach, preach, pray, praise God, sing hymns, and offer words of love, hope, and peace to those around us.

Yes, speech is like fire, a good servant but a terrible master. How, then, can we determine that our speech will be a blessing and not a curse? The Psalmist vowed, "I will take heed to my ways that I sin not with my tongue" (Psalm 39:1). Luther reminds us, "The tongue of a Christian is ruled only with the bridle of faith and love."

HIS VERY OWN

I keep asking that the God of our Lord Jesus Christ, the glorious Father, may give you the Spirit of wisdom and revelation, so that you may know Him better.

—Ephesians 1:17 NIV

In the Christian year, Trinity Sunday is always the first Sunday after Pentecost. Pentecost is the seventh Sunday after Easter. Pentecost Sunday, of course, commemorates the gift of the Holy Spirit on that memorable occasion recorded in Acts 2. It is appropriate, therefore, that following the observance of that event there should be an occasion in the church calendar to honor the Trinity—Father, Son, and Holy Spirit. Of course, we should honor the Trinity in every service of the church.

Dr. Augustus Hopkins Strong, a Baptist theologian, has maintained that the doctrine of the Trinity furnishes the key to all other doctrines. That is not difficult to demonstrate. The very first verse in the Bible anticipates the Trinity. "In the beginning God created the heavens and the earth." The word which is translated "God" in this verse is "Elohim," which is a plural word. Yet, it could not be translated "gods" since the first tenet of the Hebrew religion is "The Lord our God is one God." That fact implies what the Bible explicitly teaches elsewhere, that the members of the Trinity—Father, Son, and Holy Spirit—were each involved in the creation of the universe.

What is true of the doctrine of creation is also true of the doctrine of redemption. We see that in this passage of Scripture where Paul expounds and extols that great truth of the Bible. In verses 3 and 4 he speaks of the work of the Father in our salvation. In verses 5 through 7 he explains the part that Christ played, and in verses 13 and 14 he explains the place of the Holy Spirit in our Christian experience. There is a gospel chorus based on this passage of Scripture that expresses it so well:

His very own, His very own,
Wonderful grace in His word is made known;
Chosen by the Father;
Purchased by the Son;
Sealed with the Spirit;
I'm His very own.

(Sidney E. Cox, "His Very Own")

JUSTICE AND MERCY

He has showed you, O man, what is good. And what does the LORD require of you? To act justly and to love mercy and to walk humbly with your God.

—Micah 6:8 NIV

In writing about his days as a parochial high school student in Buffalo, New York, newsman Tim Russert tells of a day when he played hooky. It seems that one of the priests at the school knew about Tim's favorite hangout and so went looking for him in the city. When the priest found the prodigal son, he grabbed him by the collar and slammed him up against the wall.

Russert cried out, "Mercy, Father."

The priest replied, "Mercy is for God. I'm for justice."

Fortunately for Tim and for us there is a place where mercy and justice meet. That place is the cross.

Mercy there was great, and grace was free;
Pardon there was multiplied to me;
There my burdened soul found liberty, at Calvary.
(William R. Newell, "At Calvary")

"For what the law was powerless to do in that it was weakened by the sinful nature, God did by sending his own Son in the likeness of sinful man to be a sin offering. And so He condemned sin in sinful man in order that the righteous requirements of the law might be fully met in us, who do not live according to the sinful nature but according to the Spirit." (Romans 8:3-4 NIV)

Almighty and most merciful God, who knowest the thoughts of our hearts: We confess that we have sinned against thee, and done evil in thy sight. We have transgressed thy holy laws; we have neglected thy Word and ordinances. Forgive us, O Lord, we beseech thee; and give us grace and power to put away all hurtful things, that, being delivered from the bondage of sin, we may bring forth fruit worthy of repentance, and henceforth may ever walk in thy holy ways; through Jesus Christ our Lord. Amen.

WISDOM OF MY FATHER

If you, then, though you are evil, know how to give good gifts to your children, how much more will your Father in heaven give good gifts to those who ask him!

—Matthew 7:11 NIV

After reading *Big Russ and Me*, I felt compelled to read *Wisdom of Our Fathers*. *Wisdom of Our Fathers* is a selection from more than 30,000 letters received by Tim Russert, moderator of *Meet the Press*, to Tim's best seller, *Big Russ and Me*. I decided that I needed to write about the wisdom of my father.

Oddly enough, most of my happy memories of my father have to do with the outdoors. Perhaps it's because his happiest moments seemed to be outdoors. He said to me once as we left the parking lot at the Quaker Oats plant where he worked for more than thirty-five years, "It's just like being in prison."

I remember going late at night with him into the woods behind our house to give his hunting dogs some exercise. I usually carried the kerosene lantern and would often fall asleep when we stopped for the dogs to find us. In our daytime walks in those same woods he showed me how to identify the tracks of different animals: rabbits, squirrels, skunks, quail, fox, etc. Then there were those fishing trips for bullheads and blue gills at Patchin's Pond. Dad was Scoutmaster of Troop 55, so there were numerous camping trips and swims in Indian Creek.

But the incident I cherish the most had to do with my attempt to earn some money by trapping wild animals and selling their hides. I put a trap in a little cave in the dump where the farmer hauled his garbage. My dad seemed to take great interest in my venture into trapping. Each afternoon after school I would inspect the trap. Each day for several days I came up empty.

Then one day—success at last—a possum. It never occurred to me to question why the animal was dead. Sometime later my mother told me that my dad had shot the animal the night before and the next day walked a mile each way to put the animal in my trap. I was disappointed that I was not the great trapper I thought I was, but over the years I have come to realize what a great father I had.

"Behold, what manner of love the father has bestowed on us that we should be called the children of God" (1 John 3:1).

CHRISTIANITY IN ACTION

Show me your faith without your works, and I will show you my faith by my works.

—James 2:18b NKJV

A group of high school students was interviewing Supreme Court Justice Oliver Wendell Holmes. Holmes asked the group, "What are you doing in Washington?"

One of the students replied, "We've come to see the government in action."

The quick-witted Holmes responded, "Is that one word or two words?"

As people observe your life and mine do they see Christianity in action or Christianity inaction? The order of worship in one church bulletin describes well the average American churchgoer: "Rise Up, O Man of God" (the congregation will remain seated).

There is a story about Erwin Rommel, the famous German general in World War II. When he was inspecting the west wall, the gigantic fortification in Normandy intended to thwart the allied invasion in June, 1944, Rommel came across a group of workers stringing barbed wire. They were being supervised by a young lieutenant wearing white gloves watching the other men work. Rommel walked up to the officer and ordered him to remove his gloves. Fortunately for the lieutenant his hands were cut and bleeding so that he could not help string the wire. Maybe instead of singing "Will There Be Any Stars in My Crown?" we should be singing "Will There Be Any Scars on My Hands?"

"Show me your faith without works and I will show you my faith by my works" (James 2:18).

NOTABLE SAYINGS ABOUT THE BIBLE

Your word is a lamp to my feet and a light for my path.
—Psalm 119:105 NIV

"I believe the Bible is the best gift God has ever given to man. All the good from the Savior of the world is communicated to us through this book."

—Abraham Lincoln

"I have known ninety-five of the world's great men in my time, and of those eighty-seven were followers of the Bible."

—W. E. Gladstone

"It is impossible to rightly govern the world without God and the Bible."

—George Washington

"Whatever merit there is in anything that I have written is simply due to the fact that when I was a child my mother daily read me a part of the Bible and daily made me learn a part of it by heart."

—John Ruskin

"The Bible is worth all other books which have ever been printed."

—Patrick Henry

"The Bible is the sheet-anchor of our liberties."

—U. S. Grant

"That book, sir, is the rock on which our republic rests."

—Andrew Jackson

"In all my perplexities and distresses, the Bible has never failed to give me light and strength."

—*Robert E. Lee*

"Bible reading is an education in itself."

—*Lord Tennyson*

"The New Testament is the very best book that ever was or ever will be known in the world."

—*Charles Dickens*

"There are more sure marks of authenticity in the Bible than in any secular history."

—*Sir Isaac Newton*

ALL THINGS TOGETHER

We know that in all things God works for the good of those who love Him, who have been called according to His purpose.
—Romans 8:28 NIV

John Foster Dulles served as Secretary of State during the Eisenhower administration. Dulles was a devout Christian and a member of the Board of Foreign Missions of the Presbyterian Church. His brother had served for many years as a missionary to China.

Secretary Dulles said once that when things were at an impasse during the difficult days of the Cold War that he would go off by himself and meditate on these words of Romans 8:28 to see if there was some way in which he was missing God's purpose. Invariably, he came away with new insight and clearer vision.

O Word of God incarnate, O wisdom from on high,
O Truth unchanged, unchanging, O light of our dark sky;
We praise Thee for the radiance that from the hallowed page,
A lantern to our footsteps, Shines on from age to age.
(William W. How, "O Word of God Incarnate")

Almighty and most merciful God, we give thanks to Thee for the light of another day, for the work we have to do, and for the strength to do it. Guide us, we pray Thee, by Thy truth; uphold us by Thy power; and purify us by the continual indwelling of Thy Spirit. Grant that in every circumstance we may grow in wisdom, and knowing the things that belong to our peace, obtain strength to persevere; through Jesus Christ our Lord. Amen.

SEARCH ME, O GOD

Search me, O God, and know my heart; test me and know my anxious thoughts. See if there is any offensive way in me, and lead me in the way everlasting.

—Psalm 139:23-24 NIV

A physician had sent me for a chest x-ray. Later in going over the results, he asked me if I had ever worked around chickens. I thought that was a rather strange question but, as a matter of fact, when I was a boy my parents raised chickens. It was my duty to gather the eggs and provide food and water for a hundred or so chickens. The doctor explained that I had scar tissue on my lungs left by a micro-organism carried by chickens. Even though that problem had long since been alleviated, the scar tissue remained in its identifiable pattern. I was amazed that the doctor could tell me something that had happened to me over sixty years before. How like the all-knowing God who knows my life from its beginning to its ending.

For a spiritual x-ray try this: Read each of the Ten Commandments in turn and after each pray the words of Psalm 139:23-24. For example, the First Commandment says, "You shall have no other gods before me" (Exod. 20:3).

"Search me, O God, and know my heart: try me and know my thoughts: and see if there be any wicked way in me, and lead me in the way everlasting" (Psalm 139:23-24).

And then pray the words of Psalm 51:1-2: "Have mercy on me, O God, according to thy loving kindness; according unto the multitude of thy tender mercies blot out my transgressions. Wash me thoroughly from my iniquity and cleanse me from my sin."

In a chapel service at Northern Baptist Seminary, I heard J. Edwin Orr, Oxford graduate and itinerant evangelist, tell of an experience he had in Australia. He was feeling very depressed and sat on a park bench to meditate. In less than a half hour he wrote four verses of the hymn "Search Me, O God" based on Psalm 139:23-24.

Search me, O God, and know my heart today;
Try me, O Savior, know my thoughts, I pray.
See if there be some wicked way in me;
Cleanse me from every sin and set me free.

SPREADING THE WORD

His delight is in the law of the Lord.

—Psalm 1:2a NIV

Lee Gard was a deacon in the first church that I served in Rockford, Illinois. He also taught the adult Sunday school class. Like the godly man described in Psalm 1, his delight was in the law of the Lord.

Lee worked in the cost accounting department of one of the large factories in the city. He once described his job as "a pressure cooker." People constantly called on him for cost estimates and, of course, everyone wanted their information immediately. An error in his calculations could cost the company thousands of dollars.

Lee developed a technique for keeping his head in the whirl of activity around him. Before he began his work each day he would write a verse of Scripture at the top of his appointment calendar, a different verse each day. He would look at that verse several times during the day and would often memorize the verse that he had written. It seemed always to give him the inner strength that he needed for his job.

Lee's practice had an interesting sidelight. One day one of his coworkers saw the Scripture verse and asked about it. Lee explained what it was and why he had written it there. After that this coworker would come every day and read the verse for the day. Soon other workers in the department would come to Lee's desk and read the verse, and later even workers from other departments came to read it. Like the man in the Psalm, Lee brought forth fruit in his season.

THE CROWN OF LIFE

Be faithful, even to the point of death, and I will give you the crown of life.

—Revelation 2:10c NIV

Martha was a deaconess in our first church in Rockford, Illinois. Like many of the people in that church she was a Swedish immigrant. If I ever knew a person who had the gift of hospitality, Martha was that person. Whenever we had a guest speaker, she would always volunteer to have the preacher to Sunday dinner. Not only that, she also invited the pastor and his family, as well. Our boys were always delighted to hear that we were going to Martha Johnson's for Sunday dinner because Martha Johnson's Swedish meatballs were "out of this world."

When interviewing Martha as the "Member of the Month" for our church newsletter, I discovered that her favorite Bible verse was Revelation 2:10—"Be thou faithful until death and I will give thee a crown of life." When the church celebrated its twenty-fifth anniversary, I was the guest speaker and took the opportunity to visit Martha in the nursing home where she had lived for several years. She had suffered a stroke and was completely paralyzed on one side of her body. Nevertheless, I found her to be the same joyous Christian I had known so many years before. The words of an old Swedish hymn speak of Martha.

Neither life nor death shall ever
From the Lord His children sever;
Unto them His grace He showeth,
And their sorrows all He knoweth.

Though He giveth or He taketh,
God His children ne'er forsaketh,
His the loving purpose solely
To preserve them pure and holy.
                    (Lina Sandell, "Children of the Heavenly Father")

OUR TROUBLESHOOTER

God is our refuge and strength, a very present help in trouble.

—Psalm 46:1

This mighty affirmation of faith was composed to commemorate the miraculous deliverance of the city of Jerusalem from the Assyrian army of Sennacharib. Three times in Psalm 46 God is spoken of as our refuge. The word which is translated "refuge" in verse one literally means "fortress." God is our fortress and strength. The psalmist's meaning is quite clear. The city of Jerusalem was a fortress. It had a high wall around it just as does modern Jerusalem. The wall was some thirty-five feet high in places. The purpose of the wall was, of course, to provide protection from the enemy in time of war. The wall had served that purpose well in the siege of Jerusalem by the Assyrians. So, you see, the writer is saying that just as the wall of Jerusalem protected the inhabitants from the attacking Assyrians on that occasion, so the loving arms of God afford protection to all those who flee to Him in time of trouble.

Martin Luther was one who learned that lesson well. On one occasion when he had first begun preaching justification by faith, he received a letter from one of the most powerful men in Europe. The letter read, "Martin Luther, if you do not desist in your false teaching, I will gather together all of the armies of Europe and send them against you and then where will you be, Martin Luther?" Luther sent back this glorious reply: "Right where I am now; safe in the hands of God." It was in that same spirit that Luther wrote his great hymn "A Mighty Fortress Is Our God."

A mighty fortress is our God,
A bulwark never failing:
Our helper He amid the flood
Of mortal ills prevailing.

VAIN REPETITIONS

But when ye pray, use not vain repetitions as the heathen do.
—Matthew 6:7

It was the custom at Loyola University in Chicago for the professor to lead the class in the recitation of the Lord's Prayer at the beginning of the first class of each day. There was one professor who resented this intrusion on his class time. It is said that he began reciting the Lord's Prayer as he walked through the door of the classroom and completed it by the time he reached the lectern. That, I would say, is an example of vain repetition.

There are some sincere Christians who refuse to recite the Lord's Prayer because they feel that it is a violation of Jesus' prohibition against vain repetition in our prayers. It should be pointed out, however, that Jesus recited prayers. On the cross he cried, "My God, my God, why have you forsaken me?" (Matt. 27:46). This is a quotation from the prayer found in Psalm 22. There were certain prayers that every devout Jew was required to recite daily. There can be little doubt but that Jesus learned those prayers as a boy and recited them each day all of his life.

These words of Jesus are not so much a condemnation of repetition as they are of vanity. "And when you pray, you must not be like the hypocrites; for they love to stand and pray...that they may be seen by men" (Matt. 6:5 RSV). There is pride of place, pride of face, pride of race, but worst of all is pride of grace. Jesus told of two men who went up to the temple to pray. The Pharisee prayed, "God, I thank thee that I am not like other men, extortioners, unjust, adulterers, or even like this tax collector" (Luke 18:11). The tax collector simply prayed, "God, be merciful to me a sinner" (Luke 18:13b). Referring to the tax collector Jesus said, "I tell you that this man was justified rather than the other" (Luke 18:14a).

What distinguishes true prayer is that it is offered to God and not to men. A certain great preacher once described an ornate and elaborate prayer offered in a Boston church as the most eloquent prayer ever offered to a Boston audience. The preacher was much more concerned with impressing the congregation than with making contact with God.

In 1885 D. L. Moody was holding a tent meeting in London. Out of curiosity a young man entered the tent and sat down, only to find himself listening to a long and tedious prayer by one of the speakers. The young man was bored and was about to leave when D. L. Moody stood up and said to the audience, "Let us sing a hymn while our brother finishes his prayer." The young man was so impressed that he decided to remain in the meeting. That meeting changed his life. That young man was Wilfred Grenfell who later became the famous missionary doctor to Labrador. Prayer is not eloquence but earnestness.

HEALTH AND WEALTH

Consider it pure joy, my brothers, whenever you face trials of many kinds, because you know that the testing of your faith develops perseverance.
—James 1:2-3 NIV

A deacon was complaining to his pastor about what he considered the injustice of God. The deacon said, "I'm a deacon in the church; I teach Sunday school. I give a tenth of all that I earn. Yet, when times are hard I'm the one who gets laid off. It's my kids who get sick. My neighbor is a boozer and a womanizer. He never loses his job. His kids never get sick. It just isn't fair. I don't understand."

The pastor replied, "I think it's like this. The devil knows he's got your neighbor. He's just not sure about you!"

Believe it or not but that deacon is still with us in the form of the health and wealth gospel. There are those who believe that if you are a Christian and living for the Lord that He will give you health and wealth to the degree of your faithfulness.

The book of Job deals with this subject. Job lost all of his worldly possessions in a natural disaster. His children were killed at the same time. His wife turned against him, saying, "Curse God and die" (2:9). As Job sat on an ash heap, his body covered with hideous sores, three of his friends came to comfort him. They said, "Job, the reason that these things have happened to you is because of some secret sin in your life. If you confess that sin, God will heal you."

Job knew that this was not so, and at last he could say to his friends of his relation to His God, "Though He slay me, yet still will I trust Him" (Job 13:15).

O for a faith that will not shrink
Though pressed by many a foe,
That will not tremble on the brink
Of any earthly woe;

That will not murmur nor complain
Beneath the chast'ning rod,
But in the hour of grief or pain
Will lean upon its God.
    (William H. Bathurst, "O for a Faith That Will Not Shrink")

SLAVES OF CHRIST

You were bought at a price; do not become slaves of men.
—1 Corinthians 7:23 NIV

In the ancient Greek world, it was possible for a slave at a great effort to purchase his own freedom. This was how he did it. In the little spare time he had, he took odd jobs to earn some money, however little. His master had the right to claim commission even on these poor earnings. But the slave would deposit everything he could earn in this way in the temple of some god. When—it might be after several years—he had his complete purchase price laid up in the temple, he would take his master there, the priest would hand over the money, and then symbolically the slave became the property of the god and therefore free of all human bondage. That is what Paul is thinking of. Christians have been purchased by Christ; therefore, no matter what their human status may be, they are free of all slavery to others because they are the property of Christ.

My life, my love I give to Thee
Thou Lamb of God who died for me;
Oh, may I ever faithful be,
My Saviour and my God!

I'll live for Him who died for me,
How happy then my life shall be!
I'll live for Him who died for me,
My Saviour and my God.

(Ralph H. Hudson, "I'll Live For Him")

WHEN THE BLUE JAY DIED

Are not two sparrows sold for a penny? Yet not one of them will fall to the ground apart from the will of your Father.

—Matthew 10:29 NIV

One day when grandson Sean was in the first grade, he came home from school and told his mother that school would be dismissed early the next day because the Blue Jay died. His mother thought that was rather strange. She questioned Sean as to what the teacher had actually said, but he insisted that was what the teacher had said. Sean's mother decided that she had better consult a higher authority and so she called the school and talked to the principal. When she told the principal what Sean had said he had a good laugh. He then explained that the Roman Catholic Cardinal in the city had died and the funeral procession would be going right by the school at about the time school was ordinarily dismissed, so it seemed a wise thing to dismiss the students early that day. That story has become a part of our family lore. Though it happened many years ago it still brings a chuckle whenever it is mentioned.

There is also a profound truth in that otherwise humorous incident. Only a little child could have such faith to believe that the death of a Blue Jay would justify an early dismissal from school. Little wonder that Jesus said that a little child should be greatest in the Kingdom of Heaven. He also said, "Except you be converted and become as little children you shall not enter the Kingdom of Heaven" (Matt. 18:3). And again He declared, "Not one sparrow falls to the ground but your heavenly Father sees it" and "You are of much more value than many sparrows" (Matt. 10:31).

If the Father's eye is on the sparrow,
Then I know He cares for me.

125

SHE SHOOTS; HE SCORES

Be kind and compassionate to one another, forgiving each other, just as in Christ God forgave you.

—Ephesians 4:32 NIV

Jeff was an eleven-year-old African-American boy who lived on the south side of Chicago. He had been declared a juvenile delinquent by Family Court because of his chronic truancy. He had previously been sent to the county residential school for truants three times and was now on probation.

Suddenly, Jeff started attending school regularly. His probation officer was curious about the explanation for Jeff's sudden about-face. Jeff seemed such an unlikely candidate for truancy. For one thing, he had two parents living together, something that was hardly ever true of juvenile delinquents in that area. Furthermore, he lived right across the street from the school!

In his attempt to discover the reason for Jeff's turnaround, the probation officer interviewed a number of people, beginning with Jeff. He paid a visit to Jeff's school and asked to see Jeff. A few minutes later Jeff walked into the office carrying a basketball. The principal, Miss Martin, a tall, trim African-American lady, called to Jeff from the other side of the counter, "Hey, Jeff, let me have it." Jeff threw the ball to her and she threw it back to him. After several passes back and forth, Jeff ended up with the basketball!

The probation officer and Jeff went out and sat down on a bench outside of the office. The officer asked, "How come you're carrying your basketball in school?"

Jeff answered, "Oh, it's not mine. It belongs to the school. Miss Martin told me that as long as I stay in school, I can take the ball home and come back after school and shoot baskets in the school yard."

There was the answer! A few ounces of rubber filled with air had completely changed a boy's life! A reminder of how little it takes to change a child's behavior—a smile, a compliment, a pat on the back. "Kindness is to do and say the kindest thing in the kindest way" (McGuffeys' Reader).

IMMORTALITY

I give them eternal life, and they shall never perish; no one can snatch them out of my hand.

—John 10:28 NIV

In modern thought several ways of conceiving immortality have been distinguished. Biological immortality is basic. Parents live on in their offspring. We live on in our children and later descendants. A second kind of immortality is that of influence, or social immortality. What we do and say lives after us. Another kind of immortality is conceivable. It is usually called impersonal immortality. The belief is that we may not go on after death as separate, individual persons, but are absorbed back again into the Universal Life, or God, from which we came.

But what is commonly meant by immortality is the individual personal continuance of each person beyond physical death. For persons to whom Christian faith is meaningful, the historic argument may be strong. The Christian religion has taught that Jesus arose from the dead and entered upon the everlasting life in the presence of God. A closely related argument bases belief in immortality upon the assurances of the Bible. On the assumption that the Bible is an inspired and authoritative book, what are understood to be its teachings about this subject are accepted as true and final. Another argument is that which bases the belief in immortality upon faith in the existence and nature of God. If God is, and is the kind of God that religious persons usually believe Him to be, then personal continuance for believers seems more likely.

Tell me not in mournful numbers
Life is but an empty dream;
For the soul is dead that slumbers,
And things are not what they seem.

No, life is real, Life is earnest;
And the grave is not its goal.
Dust to dust to dust returneth,
Was not spoken of the soul.
                  (Henry Wadsworth Longfellow, from "A Psalm of Life")

MIXED MESSAGES

I am torn between the two: I desire to depart and be with Christ, which is better by far; but it is more necessary for you that I remain in the body.

—Philippians 1:23-24 NIV

A man knelt to pray in church. As he prayed, a member of the church knelt beside him and whispered, "Hang on, brother, hang on." The man continued to pray and a few minutes later another member knelt on the other side and whispered, "Let go, brother, let go." The man said that in trying to decide whether to hang on or let go he nearly missed the blessing of God!

The Christian traveling through this world often receives mixed messages. Determining which voice to obey is not an easy task. Facing the prospect of the cross, Jesus sweat great drops of blood as he prayed, "Not my will but Thine be done" (Luke 22:42). Writing from his Roman imprisonment, the apostle Paul struggled with the desire to depart this life to be with Christ and his wish to remain alive and minister to his friends on earth. "I am torn between the two: I desire to depart and be with Christ, which is better by far; but it is more necessary for you that I remain in the body" (Phil. 1:23-24 NIV).

What is one to do? James advises, "If any of you lacks wisdom, he should ask God, who gives generously to all without finding fault, and it will be given to him" (James 1:5 NIV).

Give me the courage to change those things which can be changed; the patience to accept those things which cannot be changed; and the wisdom to know the difference.

(Reinhold Niebuhr, "Serenity Prayer")

THE UNITY OF THE SPIRIT

There are different kinds of gifts, but the same Spirit.
—1 Corinthians 12:4 NIV

Denominationalism is thought by some to be the blight of the Christian church. Personally, I think that the differences in our denominations are not nearly as great or as important as we have been led to believe. Another thing that we learn is that our differences are not necessarily a hindrance but a help. Now to be sure, our differences can be a hindrance to the work of God. In the first chapter of First Corinthians Paul chastises the believers in that church for their divisive spirit. Some said, "We follow Paul." Others said, "We follow Peter." Still others said, "We follow Apollos." It is this divisive spirit that has so often brought the church into disrepute in the eyes of many outside the church.

On the other hand our differences can be an asset in the service of God. P. K. Wrigley said, "If two men in any organization agree about everything one of them isn't necessary." When someone suggested to Abraham Lincoln that there were too many denominations, he replied, "My good brother, you are all wrong. The more denominations we have the better. They are all getting somebody in that the others could not and even with the numerous divisions, we are doing tolerably well."

In the passage that follows this one, Paul compares the church to a human body. What he says is that it is the diversity in the church that is its strength. An eye is not an ear. A hand is not a foot. In fact, someone has suggested that the various denominations represent the various parts of the body of Christ. The Roman Catholics who emphasize beauty in worship are the eyes of Christ. The Congregationalists who listen to the voice of the people are the ears of Christ. The Presbyterians who have placed great emphasis on education are the mind of Christ.

The Lutherans who emphasize preaching are the voice of Christ. The Methodists who have shown great concern for the needy are the hands of Christ. And the Baptists who have led in the world missionary enterprise are the feet of Christ. As Paul says, "There are different kinds of gifts but one Spirit." So to all of our Christian brothers and sisters in other denominations let us say, "You go to your church and I'll go to mine but let's walk along together." "Make every effort to keep the unity of the Spirit through the bond of peace" (Eph. 4:3 NIV).

A-BRAGGIN' ON JESUS

I will praise the LORD all my life; I will sing praise to my God as long as I live.

—Psalm 146:2 NIV

Vance Havner was a popular evangelist, Bible teacher, conference speaker, and devotional writer. He began preaching at the age of thirteen. Although he had only an eighth grade education, he was an eloquent preacher and a talented writer. He was still preaching when he was well over eighty years of age.

One day at a conference he met a fellow evangelist who assumed that Havner must now be retired. He asked the old preacher, "Well, what are you doing these days, Vance?"

Havner replied, "O, I'm a-doin' what I've always been a-doin'; goin' up and down the countryside a-braggin' on Jesus."

I love to tell the story of unseen things above,
Of Jesus and His glory, Of Jesus and His love.
I love to tell the story, Because I know 'tis true;
It satisfies my longings As nothing else can do.

I love to tell the story, 'Tis pleasant to repeat
What seems, each time I tell it, More wonderfully sweet,
I love to tell the story, For some have never heard
The message of salvation From God's own Holy Word.

(A. Catherine Hankey, "I Love to Tell the Story")

THE GOD OF HEALING

And the prayer offered in faith will make the sick person well; the Lord will raise him up. If he has sinned, he will be forgiven.

—James 5:15 NIV

Each branch of the United States Army has its own lapel insignia. For the infantry, it is crossed rifles. A cannon identifies a member of the artillery while the medical corps is represented by a serpent wrapped around a pole.

The serpent on the pole comes to us from the ancient Greek world. Asclepios was the Greek god of healing. His temple was in Pergamum. Located here was one of the Christian churches that the author of the biblical book of Revelation addresses. This pagan temple was the closest thing we have to a hospital in the ancient world. Thousands of people came to Pergamum to be healed and many were healed. Pergamum has been called the Lourdes of the ancient world.

Pergamum was also the government administrative center for the region. All of the residents in the area were required to make a yearly appearance in the temple and declare "Caesar is Lord." Christians refused to do that and as a consequence many of them were put to death. That is why the writer of Revelation refers to Pergamum as "The Seat of Satan."

There is a serpent on a pole mentioned elsewhere in the Bible. It has no relation to the Greek god. At one point in their sojourn from Egypt to the Promised Land the Israelites were attacked by deadly serpents and many people died. God instructed Moses to make a brass replica of a serpent and hang it on a pole. If anyone was bitten by one of these serpents and looked at the brazen serpent, they would not die.

Jesus referred to this miracle in his conversation with Nicodemus recorded in John's Gospel. Jesus said, "...as Moses lifted up the serpent in the wilderness even so must the Son of Man be lifted up" (John

3:14). He was speaking of His death on the cross. Then Jesus said, in what has been described as the Bible in one verse, "For God so loved the world that He gave His one and only Son, that whoever believes in Him shall not perish but have eternal life" (John 3:16 NIV).

> While life's dark maze I tread,
> And griefs around me spread,
> Be Thou my guide;
> Bid darkness turn to day,
> Wipe sorrow's tears away,
> Nor let me ever stray
> From Thee aside.
>
> (Ray Palmer, "My Faith Looks Up to Thee")

IS THANKSGIVING A RELIGIOUS HOLIDAY?

Enter His gates with thanksgiving and His courts with praise; give thanks to Him and praise His name.

—Psalm 100:4 NIV

On one occasion while I was serving as a pastor in Rockford, Illinois, a rather interesting discussion developed one year in the November meeting of the ministerial association. It seems that Santa Claus was scheduled to arrive at the airport on Thanksgiving Day morning. Some of the ministers were upset because their churches had planned Thanksgiving services for that same time. These pastors wanted the ministers to pass a resolution urging the Chamber of Commerce to arrange for Santa to arrive in the afternoon of Thanksgiving Day.

In the discussion that followed a Methodist minister spoke in opposition to the resolution saying, "Thanksgiving really isn't a religious holiday." Well, as you can imagine, that statement set off quite a furor. What the minister meant was that Thanksgiving is a national holiday rather than part of the Christian year in the same sense as Christmas and Easter.

However, when President Abraham Lincoln issued the first National Thanksgiving Proclamation in 1863, he called upon people "to give thanks to the Most High God for singular deliverance and blessings." Thanksgiving Day is a religious holiday to those who pause to remember Him from whom all blessings flow.

It is significant that Thanksgiving Day is immediately followed by the beginning of Advent when we celebrate the coming of Christ, God's greatest gift to the human race. "Thanks be unto God for His indescribable gift!" (2 Cor. 9:15 NIV).

THANK YOU, JOHN

In as much as you did it to one of the least of these my brethren, you did it to me.

—Matthew 25:40b NKJV

During the course of a series of revival meetings in a country church in the hills of Kentucky, the preacher challenged the members of the congregation to lead another person to Christ. John was a high school sophomore. He really didn't feel capable of doing that, but thought of one person with whom he might work—Clem, a retarded man in his early twenties. John spoke to Clem and Clem responded, surprised that anyone had paid any attention to him. After John had led Clem in a prayer receiving Christ as his Savior and Lord, Clem shook John's hand and said, "I want to thank you, John, I want to thank you."

Each Sunday after the service Clem would seek John out, shake his hand, and say, "I want to thank you, John, I want to thank you." Eventually John went away to college but would come home during summer vacation. Clem would find his friend, shake his hand, and say, "I want to thank you, John, I want to thank you." John decided to become a minister and enrolled in seminary but would come home occasionally. Clem would be sure to greet his old friend as usual. "I want to thank you, John, I want to thank you." John became a famous minister and president of one of the largest seminaries in the world. Nevertheless, he managed to visit that little church occasionally and there was Clem, "I want to thank you, John, I want to thank you."

Eventually John departed this life and went to be with his Lord. Clem attended the memorial service and the graveside service. After everyone else left, Clem stood alone by the graveside and said, "I want to thank you, John, I want to thank you."

In His time, God took Clem home. As he entered his new life, he was met by two persons: John and the Lord Jesus. It was Jesus who spoke, "I want to thank you, John, I want to thank you."

"Inasmuch as you did it to one of the least of these my brethren, you did it to me" (Matt. 25:40b).

HOW TO BE PERFECT

But the fruit of the Spirit is love, joy, peace, patience, kindness, goodness, faithfulness, gentleness and self-control. Against such things there is no law.

—Galatians 5:22-23 NIV

When Benjamin Franklin was a young man living in Philadelphia, he decided to try to achieve moral perfection. He drew up a list of twelve virtues with a short definition appended.

Temperance: Eat not to dullness; drink not to elevation.

Silence: Speak not but what may benefit others or yourself; avoid trifling conversation.

Order: Let all your things have their places; let each part of your business have its time.

Resolution: Resolve to perform what you ought; perform without fail what you resolve.

Frugality: Make no expense but to do good to others or yourself (i.e., waste nothing).

Industry: Lose no time; be always employed in something useful; cut off all unnecessary actions.

Sincerity: Use no hurtful deceit; think innocently and justly, and, if you speak, speak accordingly.

Justice: Wrong none by doing injuries, or omitting the benefits that are your duty.

Moderation: Avoid extremes; forbear resenting injuries so much as you think they deserve.

Cleanliness: Tolerate no uncleanliness in body, clothes, or habitation.

Tranquility: Be not disturbed at trifles, or at accidents common or unavoidable.

Chastity: Rarely use venery but for health or offspring, never to dullness, weakness, or the injury of your own or another's peace or reputation.

At the suggestion of a Quaker lady, he added humility: Imitate Jesus and Socrates.

The plan was this: spend a week concentrating on each virtue in turn, thus going through the entire list four times each year. Unfortunately, the system broke down under its own weight and Franklin gave it up.

In Galatians 5:22-23 the apostle Paul gave us such a list. He called it the fruit of the Spirit: love, joy, peace, patience, kindness, goodness, faithfulness, gentleness, and self-control. We receive those virtues when we receive Christ, who is one with the Spirit. We receive these virtues as a gift. "For it is by grace you have been saved, through faith—and this not from yourselves, it is the gift of God—not by works, so that no one can boast" (Eph. 2:8). When we receive Christ and the Holy Spirit we are declared righteous in the sight of God. That is called justification. As someone put it, to be justified means "just as if I'd not sinned."

Then we spend the rest of our earthly pilgrimage bringing those things into our daily lives as we come into the fullness of the stature of Christ. That is called sanctification, "the Christianizing of the Christian."

Thy Holy Spirit, Lord, alone can turn our hearts from sin;
His pow'r alone can sanctify and keep us pure within.
Thy Holy Spirit, Lord, can give the grace we need this hour;
And while we wait, O Spirit come in sanctifying pow'r.
(Henrietta E. Blair, "The Holy Spirit, Lord, Alone")

THE COMING OF THE MESSIAH

But you, Bethlehem Ephrathah, though you are small among the clans of Judah, out of you will come for me one who will be ruler over Israel, whose origins are from of old, from ancient times.

—Micah 5:2 NIV

For centuries the Jewish people waited for the coming of the messiah. The word "messiah" is a Hebrew word which means "anointed one." In ancient Israel prophets, priests, and kings were anointed with oil when they assumed office, symbolizing God's blessing upon their service. In that sense they were messiahs.

After many centuries the Jewish people began to look for THE MESSIAH, one who would be prophet, priest, and king and the Son of God. In the books of the prophets, for example, written several centuries before Christ, there are references to this coming Messiah. Isaiah wrote of the manner of his birth: "Therefore the Lord himself will give you a sign: The virgin will be with child and will give birth to a son, and will call him Immanuel" (Isaiah 7:14 NIV). Micah spoke of the place of his birth: "But you, Bethlehem Ephrathah, though you are small among the clans of Judah, out of you will come for me one who will be ruler over Israel, whose origins are from of old, from ancient times" (Micah 5:2). And there are many other such prophecies.

Of course, Christians believe that Jesus is that Messiah. The Greek word "Christos," from which we get our English word "Christ," is the equivalent of the Hebrew word "Messiah." In his great confession Peter said to Jesus, "You are the Christ [Messiah], the Son of the living God" (Matt. 16:16).

As we observe the Advent season each year that same spirit of hope and faith should prevail in the hearts and minds of all Christians.

O Holy Child of Bethlehem, descend to us we pray:
Cast out our sin and enter in: be born in us today.
>   (Phillips Brooks, "O Little Town of Bethlehem")

LET US ADORE HIM

Yet a time is coming and has now come when the true worshipers will worship the Father in spirit and truth, for they are the kind of worshipers the Father seeks.

—John 4:23 NIV

Of all the beautiful hymns and carols that we sing at the Christmas season, none is more loved than *Adeste Fideles,* "O Come All Ye Faithful." It is used in the services of both Protestant and Roman Catholic churches. It has been translated into fifty-eight languages. Christians throughout the world will sing again this Christmas season: "O come, let us adore Him, Christ the Lord."

What does this mean—to adore Him? You will find two definitions for the word "adore" in the dictionary. The first definition says that adore means "to worship or honor as a deity or divine." The second states that adore means "to feel or express reverent admiration for: to regard with fervent devotion and affection."

Which definition shall we apply to Jesus Christ? Are we to worship or honor Him as deity or divine? Or are we to feel only reverent admiration for Him? It should be clear that the author of the words of this hymn invites us to worship Jesus. He speaks of Jesus as the King of Angels and the Word of the Father.

But, of course, our beliefs about Christ should, above all, be founded in the Scriptures. It should be noted in this regard that in the New Testament the same Greek word that is used to describe worship to God the Father is also applied to Jesus. In Matthew 4:10 we are reminded "to worship the Lord thy God." In John 4:23 we are told that we are to "worship the Father in spirit and in truth."

We find the writers of the New Testament using this same word when speaking of Jesus. For example, in Matthews's Gospel we are told that "there came a leper and worshiped Him." In another place

Matthew reports that "there came a certain ruler and worshiped Him." Following His resurrection this Gospel reports that the disciples "came and held Him by the feet and worshiped Him."

Of course, Christians feel and express reverent admiration for Jesus. We also regard Him with fervent devotion and affection. Above all, we worship and honor Him as divine. We mean all of these things when we sing:

O come, let us adore Him, Christ the Lord.

IMITATORS OF GOD

I have set you an example that you should do as I have done for you.
—John 13:15 NIV

Art Linkletter was right: "Kids say the darndest things." One first grade teacher was preparing her class for Grandfather's Day. She went around the class asking each student what his or her grandfather did for a living. One little boy whose grandfather was a minister couldn't remember the word for pastor and said, "My grandfather is God."

Dr. W. Robert Smith, professor of philosophy at Bethel College in St. Paul, Minnesota, said in an interview with *Christian Life* magazine, "We live in the place of our Lord in reference to our children." In his letter to the Ephesians, the apostle Paul wrote, "Be imitators of God as little children" (Eph. 6:1).

Not everyone agrees. One lady suggested to her minister that he not offer prayer to God the Father because some people in the congregation will have had a bad relationship with their father and would be "turned off." Apparently, Jesus didn't know that. When his disciples asked Him to teach them to pray, He said, "After this manner pray, Our Father, which art in heaven."

Apparently, Harry Johnson didn't know this either. He told me once that his last memory of his father was the beating he gave his mother. Did it affect Harry? Yes, it did. He started a Sunday school for children in a government housing project!

Lord, speak to me that I may speak
In living echoes of Thy tone;
As Thou hast sought, so let me seek
Thy erring children lost and lone.

O fill me with Thy fullness, Lord,
Until my very heart o'er-flow
In kindling thought and glowing word,
Thy love to tell, Thy praise to show.

(Frances R. Havergal, "Lord, Speak to Me")

WALKING THE WALK

*He has shown you, O man, what is good; And what does the L*ORD *require of you but to do justly, to love mercy, and to walk humbly with your God?*

—Micah 6:8 NKJV

A village priest in Poland was chatting with the local communist leader. The communist leader talked of growing up in the church. The priest asked him, "Are you a Christian?"

The man replied, "I'm a believing one but not a practicing one." Then he asked the priest, "Are you a communist?"

The priest replied, "I'm a practicing one, but not a believing one."

At least the two were agreed on one thing—our beliefs should determine our behavior. We must not only talk the talk, but we should also walk the walk. As James put it, "Show me your faith without your works and I will show you my faith by my works" (James 2:18 NKJV).

Unfortunately the actual behavior of people does not always correspond with their professed beliefs. As one preacher put it, "There are too many people talking about Jesus from the teeth out." The apostle Paul spoke of those "having a form of godliness but denying the power thereof" (2 Timothy 3:5).

How can we know when we are on track?

When Jesus was asked a similar question He said, "You shall love the LORD your God with all your heart, with all your soul, and with all your mind. This is the first and great commandment. And the second is like it: You shall love your neighbor as yourself. On these two commandments hang all the Law and the Prophets" (Matt. 22:37-40 NKJV).

Why waste your time in building up
A cumbrous, long and wordy creed?
Your brother give a cooling cup,
Your neighbor help when he has need,
Love God and man and carry on.

With much to do on every hand,
Why waste your time in vain dispute?
Though you for right perchance may stand,
Your stand, at that, may bear no fruit.
Love God and man and carry on.

With much that must remain in doubt,
You yet can find your part to do.
And what is there to fight about
If you to God and self are true?
Love God and man and carry on.

(E. K. Browning)

THE THIEF OF TIME

Teach us to number our days and recognize how few they are; help us to spend them as we should.

—Psalm 90:12 TLB

On one occasion a pastor announced to his congregation that he would speak the following Sunday on the subject of procrastination. He turned to one of the deacons and said, "Brother Jones, will you please tell the people what procrastination is?" Deacon Jones didn't know, but he thought he would fake it. So he said, "Pastor, procrastination is one of the fundamental doctrines of our church!" Procrastination is, of course, the tendency to keep putting things off. Maybe Deacon Jones was right. Churches do have a tendency to delay making and implementing important decisions.

Procrastination is such a common human failing that it has been the subject of much humor. One fellow revised Benjamin Franklin's admonition, "Do not put off until tomorrow what you can do today." He said, "Do not put off until tomorrow what you can put off until the day after tomorrow." At home I have a round coaster for my coffee cup with the word "tuit" printed on it. It is for people who are always saying, "I'll do it when I get around to it." I'm not sure, but I suspect that it was given to me by my wife.

There is a tragic side to procrastination as well. At Kadesh-Barnea the children of Israel disobeyed God and postponed their decision to enter the Promised Land and, as a consequence, were condemned to wander in the desert for thirty-nine years. Almost all of those people died without seeing the Promised Land. Little wonder that Joshua said to the new generation of Israelites encamped on the east bank of the Jordan River, the edge of the Promised Land, "Choose you this day whom you will serve" (Josh. 24:15c).

One of the great heroes of American Baptists, Dr. Russell Conwell served concurrently for forty years as pastor of the great Baptist Temple in Philadelphia and president of a great university. It is incredible to think that a man could serve so successfully in two such demanding positions at the same time. Much of Russell Conwell's success was due to a three-word motto that he kept on his desk at all times, "Do it now."

That does not mean that we are to act immediately on every impulse that enters our minds. If we do that, we become like Don Quixote who mounted his horse and rode off in all directions at the same time. But when we know that something needs to be done and the time is ripe, we need to seize the moment and strike while the iron is hot. Otherwise the opportunity may be lost forever. God has said, "My Spirit will not contend with man forever, for he is mortal" (Gen. 6:3 NIV). "Behold, now is the accepted time; now is the day of salvation" (2 Cor. 6:2b).

GIVING YOUR BEST

I press on toward the goal to win the prize for which God has called me heavenward in Christ Jesus.

—Philippians 3:14 NIV

If you saw the movie *Chariots of Fire*, you may recall that it was about two British subjects who were rivals for the gold medals in the 100-meter and 200-meter runs in the 1924 Olympics. Have you ever wondered about the American contenders in those races? As a matter of fact, America's best prospect for Gold Medals in those events did not compete in the Olympics. His name was Leonard Paulu. He was a teacher and track coach at my alma mater, McKinley High School in Cedar Rapids, Iowa.

When he graduated from high school, Paulu enrolled in Grinnell College, a small school near Des Moines founded by the Congregational church. When the United States entered World War I in 1917 he interrupted his education and enlisted. He went to France with the American Expeditionary Force and was severely wounded in the battle of St. Mihiel, receiving shrapnel wounds in his head and right leg.

After his discharge from the army he returned to Grinnell to continue his education. He would graduate Phi Beta Kappa. He proved to be a superior athlete as well. In 1922 he won the National Collegiate Athletic Association championship in the 100-yard dash, and in 1923 he won both the 100-yard and the 220-yard NCAA Championships. Had he competed in the 1924 Olympics he would quite likely have won a medal and possibly a gold. Why did he not compete? By that time he was married and could not afford to make the trip to the trials. You might say that he exchanged a gold medal for a wedding ring!

Mr. Paulu was my instructor in physics and trigonometry, but the most important lesson that I learned from him was at a track meet. It was at the Grinnell Relays in 1942. The Grinnell Relays were held each year at the college in honor of Leonard Paulu, its most famous athlete. High schools from all over Iowa sent their best athletes to compete. I was entered in the one mile run along with about forty other boys. Most of the race I was in the middle of the pack, but in the final lap I was able to overtake all but two of the other runners to finish third. After I had caught my breath I reported to Mr. Paulu in the stands. He congratulated me, told me my time for the race, and then said, "You know, Dean, you could have won that race. You had too much left." I have thought of that incident many times over the years. I have often asked myself in relation to my work as a minister, a teacher, and a college administrator, "Have I really done my best?" It is my prayer that when at last I report to the Great Coach on High that I will have so run the race of life that I will hear Him say, "Well done, you good and faithful servant, enter into the joy of your reward."

HIS MAJESTY

What is man that you are mindful of him, the son of man that you care for him?

—Psalm 8:4 NIV

When Sir Isaac Newton had completed the first reflecting telescope and looked through the eyepiece of the instrument for the first time, he saw things which no human eye had ever before seen. Excitedly, he turned to an assistant standing beside him and exclaimed, "I have just caught hold of the skirts of God."

Some twenty-seven centuries before Newton, David sat on a lonely hillside contemplating the starry heavens and experienced the same sensation as we find it recorded in Psalm 8: "O LORD, our Lord, how excellent is your name in all the earth!...When I consider Your heavens, the work of Your fingers, the moon and stars which You have ordained; what is man that You are mindful of him?" (NKJV).

The majestic nature of God is revealed in the moon and the stars. Lincoln said it well, "I can understand how a man looking down on this world can be an atheist, but I cannot understand how anyone looking up at the stars can say there is no God."

The Hebrew poets and prophets had a much more limited concept of the size of the universe than any of us and yet recognized it as an indication of the unlimited power of the Creator. In Isaiah 40 we find these words: "Lift up your eyes on high, and behold who has created these things, that bring out their host by number; He calls them all by names by the greatness of His might, for that He is strong in power; not one fails."

Our advanced knowledge of the size of the universe should give us even greater faith. Today's astronomers know that the fundamental units of the universe are the stars. The stars cluster together in systems called galaxies. We live in a galaxy called the Milky Way. All these galaxies together form part of what some astronomers call a super universe. Its dimensions are almost impossible for the average mind to grasp as it measures thousands of millions of light years. A light year is the distance that light travels in a year at the rate of 186,000 miles per second.

For most of us the attempt to comprehend the significance of such facts is well nigh overwhelming. We should be able to sympathize then with the student at Princeton who listened to a lecture on the size of the universe and then raised his hand to ask the professor, "Knowing all these things, is it still possible to believe in God?" The professor thought for a moment about that and then replied, "Well, that all depends on how big your God is."

> O Lord my God! When I in awesome wonder
> Consider all the worlds Thy hands have made.
> I see the stars, I hear the rolling thunder,
> Thy power throughout the universe displayed.
>
> Then sings my soul, my Savior God to Thee:
> HOW GREAT THOU ART! HOW GREAT THOU ART! (Carl Boberg, "How Great Thou Art," trans. from Swedish by Stuart K. Hine)

WHEN GOD SEEMS FAR AWAY

My tears have been my meat day and night, while they continually say unto me, Where is thy God?

—Psalm 42:3

The problem voiced by the psalmist in Psalms 42 and 43 is one that we all encounter at times—the feeling that God is far away. The writer of the Psalms is in exile in the region of Mt. Hermon, far from Jerusalem and the tabernacle where every devout Jew believed that God dwelt and where He could be worshiped best. In deep anguish God's servant cries out, "When can I go and meet with God?"

For us the problem is more likely to be psychological than geographical. When we experience defeat, disillusionment, and disappointment in our lives we find ourselves asking, "Where is God? How could He permit this to happen to me?" We feel alone, abandoned, and afraid. The writer expresses his feeling in these words repeated three times in these two psalms: "Why are you downcast, O my soul; Why so disturbed within me?"

We all know the feeling and its challenge to our faith. We know the problem, but what is the solution? What is the way out of despondency and despair? In these two psalms, which in many manuscripts are one, the psalmist not only poses the question, he also provides the answer. For that refrain ends with these words: "Put your hope in God, for I will yet praise Him, my Savior and my God."

Hope—that is the answer to the problems and perplexities of life. For it is impossible to live without hope. Ultimately, it is impossible to live without hope in God. Leslie Weatherhead, the famous British preacher, once said, "When the Psalmist said, 'Hope thou in God,' he gave the world the only ground of hope that exists." And so the apostle Paul wrote to the Christians at Rome, "now the God of hope fill you with all joy and peace in believing, that ye may abound in hope, through the power of the Holy Spirit" (15:13).

Would it surprise you to know that at one point in his Christian life Billy Graham felt that God was far away? He said, "Once when I was going through a dark period I prayed and prayed, but the heavens seemed to be brass. I felt as though God had disappeared and that I was alone with my trial and burden. I wrote my mother about this experience and will never forget her reply. 'Son there are many times when God withdraws to test your faith. He wants you to trust Him in the darkness. Now, son, reach up by faith in the fog and you will find that His hand will be there.' In tears I knelt by my bed and experienced an overwhelming sense of God's presence."

> I believe in the sun when it is not shining.
> I believe in love even when I feel it not.
> I believe in God even when He is silent.
>
> (Anonymous)

WHAT PRAYER CHANGES

Do not be anxious about anything, but in everything, by prayer and petition, with thanksgiving, present your requests to God.
—Philippians 4:6 NIV

Perhaps, you have seen at sometime or other a plaque containing this motto: "Prayer Changes Things." And, to be sure, prayer does change things; that is, the outward circumstances of our lives. The Bible repeatedly confirms that fact. Noah prayed and God handed him a blueprint of the ark of deliverance. Moses prayed and God delivered the Israelites from Egyptian bondage. Daniel prayed and the mouths of the lions closed.

The disciples prayed and they were filled with the Holy Spirit so that three thousand were added to the church in one day. Paul prayed and hundreds of churches were born in Asia Minor and Europe. Prayer changes things, that is, the outward circumstances of our lives.

However, it was a very wise man who observed, "Prayer changes things: especially me." That is to say, prayer not only changes the outward circumstances of our lives but our inner attitudes as well. That, it seems to me, is the great emphasis of Philippians 4:6-7, which is the heart of this passage.

Verse 6 tells us how to pray and verse 7 tells us what happens when we pray. "In everything by prayer and supplication with thanksgiving let your requests be made known unto God; and the peace of God which passes all understanding shall keep your hearts and minds through Christ Jesus."

Lord, what a change within us one short hour
Spent in Thy presence will avail to make!
What heavy burdens from our bosoms take!
What parched grounds refresh as with a shower!

161

We kneel, and all around us seems to lower;
We rise, and all, the distant and the near,
Stands forth in sunny outline, brave and clear;
We kneel, how weak! We rise, how full of power!
Why, therefore, should we do ourselves this wrong,
Or others, that we are not always strong—
That we are sometimes overborne with care—
That we should ever weak or heartless be,
Anxious or troubled—when with us is prayer
And joy and strength and courage are with Thee?
                    (Archbishop Trench, "Prevailing Prayer")

THE GREATEST OF THESE

And now abideth faith, hope, charity, these three; but the greatest of these is charity.

—1 Corinthians 13:13

"You shall love the Lord your God with all your heart and with all your soul and with all your mind and you shall love your neighbor as yourself. On these two laws hang all the law and the prophets." (Matt. 22:37-40). In these words Jesus summed up the entire Old Testament and his message as well. Jesus said that the entire message of the Bible is contained in one word: love. Elsewhere, in speaking to His disciples in that upper room, He declared, "By this, all will know that you are my disciples if you have love one to another" (John 13:35). And the apostle Paul, writing of the results of the Spirit's working in the heart of a person, lists nine virtues which he calls the fruit of the Spirit. At the head of that list is love. In 1 Corinthians 13, the great love chapter of the Bible, Paul extols love saying, "Now abides these three: faith, hope and love, but the greatest of these is love" (v. 13). No one can deny that the essence of the Christian faith and life is contained in that one word: love.

First Corinthians 13 is a love poem. In fact, it may have been an early Christian hymn. In this poem the apostle Paul extols love as the greatest of all gifts. It is the greatest gift that we can receive. It is the greatest gift that we can give. So I would say to you what Paul says in the first verse of the chapter that follows this one: follow the way of love.

To be a Christian means to be like Jesus Christ. For as the apostle Paul exhorts in Ephesians 5:1, "Be imitators of God as dearly loved children, and walk in love, even as Christ loved you and gave Himself for you." So you see, just as you can insert the name of Christ in place of love in this paragraph, you can substitute the word "Christian" in place of love.

Then the paragraph would read like this. A Christian is patient and kind; a Christian is not jealous or boastful; he or she is not arrogant or rude. A Christian does not insist on his or her own way; he or she is not irritable or resentful; he or she does not rejoice at wrong, but rejoices in the right. A Christian bears all things, believes all things, hopes all things, endures all things.

One Sunday after I had finished the children's talk, a little boy was leading his sister by the hand to children's church. As he passed me he said, "This is our sister. We love her." Then he took a couple of more steps and turned back to me and said, "And I love Jesus, too." That's it. That is the message of the Bible and of our Christian faith. That's all that we know and all that we need to know. Your are my brothers and sisters. I love you. And I love Jesus, too.

THE SECRET OF AN
UNTROUBLED HEART

Do not let your hearts be troubled. Trust in God, trust also in Me.
—John 14:1 NIV

"In my Father's house are many rooms....I am going there to prepare a place for you" (John 14:2 NIV). As Christians we find joy in the midst of trouble knowing that this life is not all nor is it the best. As Paul said, "I reckon that the sufferings of this present time are not worthy to be compared with the glory that shall be revealed in us"(Rom. 8:18).

Heaven is described in the Bible as a great kingdom. Our Lord spoke often of the Kingdom of Heaven. Peter says, "…Make your calling and election sure. For if you do these things, you will never fail, and you will receive a rich welcome into the eternal kingdom of our Lord and Savior Jesus Christ" (2 Peter 1:10-11 NIV).

Heaven is also described as a beautiful city. In the book of Revelation John writes, "I saw the Holy City, the New Jerusalem, coming down out of heaven from God, prepared as a bride beautifully dressed for her husband" (Rev. 21:2). "The wall was made of jasper, and the city of pure gold, as pure as glass. The foundations of the city walls were decorated with every kind of precious stone" (Rev. 21:18-19 NIV). How wonderful to know that your citizenship is in heaven.

But of all the beautiful descriptions of heaven in the Bible the most beautiful is in John 14. For Jesus says that heaven is like home. "In my Father's house are many rooms." The dearest spot on earth to any of us is that place we call home. There is no burden that we cannot bear if we know that at the end of the day, we can go to that place of peace and rest. For the Christian, death is simply going home and life is simply a longing to go home.

There is a beautiful scene in *Uncle Tom's Cabin* that reminds us of the comfort that our heavenly hope gives in the midst of the sufferings of this life. Because of financial reverses, Uncle Tom had been sold and separated from the family and the home that he had known all his life. Years later, hearing that the old slave was dying, his former owner finds him, intending to buy him back and let him die at home in peace. His former master enters the slave cabin and finds the old man near the point of death. He speaks: "Uncle Tom, I've come to buy you back and take you home."

The old slave opens his eyes and smiles at his beloved former owner. He replies, "You're too late, Massah George, the Lord done bought me and He's gwine take me home." "Let not your heart be troubled...In my Father's house are many rooms."

THE TRUE WAY OF LIFE

Jesus answered, "I am the Way and the Truth and the Life. No one comes to the Father except through me."

—*John 14:6* NIV

In *The Imitation of Christ* Thomas a Kempis said regarding this verse: "Without the Way there is no going; without the Truth there is no knowing; without the Life there is no living. I am the Way which you must follow, the Truth which you must believe, the Life for which you must hope." Jesus is the True Way of Life.

What does it mean to follow Christ? For one thing, it means to follow His teachings. If we say that someone is a follower of Karl Marx, we mean that the person adheres to the teachings of communism. To be a Christian, then, means to follow the teachings of Jesus Christ. Most people would agree that the Sermon on the Mount is the essence of the teachings of Jesus Christ. There we find the Beatitudes and the Lord's Prayer and many other things that are the foundation of our faith. At the conclusion of the sermon, Jesus said, "Everyone who hears these words of mine and puts them into practice is like a wise man who built his house on the rock. The rain came down, the streams rose, and the winds blew and beat against that house; yet it did not fall, because it had its foundation on the rock" (Matt. 7:24-25 NIV).

To follow Christ also means to follow His example. One of the Greek words which is translated "follow" in our English Bible is the basis of our English words "mimic" and "imitate." For example, in the King James Version Ephesians 5:1 reads, "Be followers of God as dear children" but in most modern translations it reads, "Be imitators of God as dearly loved children." To imitate God one must imitate Jesus Christ, for as Jesus says in this conversation with the disciples in John 14, "He that has seen me has seen the Father for the Father and I are one." Paul affirms that in Ephesians 5:1: "Be imitators of God, therefore, as dearly loved children and live a life of love, just as Christ loved us and gave himself up for us as a fragrant offering and sacrifice to God."

One classic devotional book is a work of fiction entitled *In His Steps*. The book, written by Charles Sheldon, was published in 1923. This little book has challenged and inspired people for over eighty years. It is a fictional account of the Rev. Henry Maxwell and the First Church of Raymond. One Sunday Rev. Maxwell preached a sermon based on the words of 1 Peter 2:21—"For hereunto were ye called; because Christ also suffered for you, leaving you an example, that you should follow his steps." A homeless man attended the church for the first time and fainted during the service. Rev. Maxwell took the man into his own home where the man died during the week. As a result of that tragedy, Rev. Maxwell preached a sermon the next Sunday in which he challenged members of his congregation to pledge to precede every action which they took in the coming year with the question "What would Jesus do?" The rest of the book tells the story of the remarkable transformation that took place in the lives of the members of that congregation and their community as they sought to follow in the steps of Jesus Christ. And what a transformation would take place in your life and mine if we were to always ask that question in every action that we take: "What would Jesus do?"

MY LIVING REDEEMER

I know that my Redeemer lives, and that in the end He will stand upon the earth. And after my skin has been destroyed, yet in my flesh I will see God.

—Job 19:25-26 NIV

Benjamin Franklin, American patriot and signer of the Declaration of Independence, left this epitaph for his tombstone: "The body of Benjamin Franklin, Printer, like the cover of an old book, its contents torn out and stript of its lettering and gilding, lies here food for worms. But the work shall not be wholly lost for it will, as he believed, appear once more in a new and more perfect edition corrected and amended by the author." And so we believe.

In 1 Corinthians 15, Paul tells us something of the nature of the resurrection body. The resurrection body is much like our natural body in many respects, for men recognized Christ, and he ate fish with his disciples. But it was a different kind of body in many other respects, for it was a body that enabled Christ to appear and disappear at will. Paul says of the resurrection body, "It is sown in corruption, it is raised in incorruption; it is sown in dishonor, it is raised in glory; it is sown in weakness, it is raised in power; it is sown a natural body, it is raised a spiritual body" (vv. 42-44).

Yes, this is the faith once delivered to the saints. "How that Christ died for our sins according to the Scriptures; and that he was buried, and that he rose again the third day according to the Scriptures…For this corruptible must put on incorruption and this mortal must put on immortality" (1 Cor. 15:3-4, 53).

On the gates of many cemeteries in England is inscribed a paraphrase of Job 19:25-26 by Isaac Watts, the great English hymn writer. I pray that they may express the faith of us all.

God my redeemer ever lives,
And often from the skies,
Looks down and watches o'er my dust,
Till He shall bid it rise.

Though greedy worms devour my skin,
And gnaw my wasting flesh,
Yet He will build my bones again,
And clothe them all afresh.

Then shall I see my Savior's face,
With strong immortal eyes,
And feast upon His unknown grace,
With rapture and surprise.

A SOUL-SEARCHING QUESTION

For what profit is it to a man if he gains the whole world, and loses his own soul?

—Matthew 16:26a NKJV

Joe, age 47, is a typical American male. His story has been told in a series of articles in *The Reader's Digest*: "I Am Joe's Heart"; "I Am Joe's Lungs"; "I Am Joe's Liver." A part of Joe is more important than any of these or all of these—that part of Joe that gives life to his body—that part of Joe that will continue to live long after Joe's heart, lungs, and liver have ceased to function. That part, of course, is Joe's immortal soul, your soul and mine.

You will look in vain in textbooks of anatomy and physiology for descriptions of the soul. In the Bible the word that is translated "soul" literally means "that which breathes" and as such distinguishes the soul from flesh. A person, then, has a twofold nature: a material nature, the body, and an immaterial nature, the soul.

Samuel Taylor Coleridge wrote, "Either we have an immortal soul or we have not. If we have not, we are beasts; the first and wisest of beasts it may be; but still beasts. We only differ in degree, and not in kind; just as the elephant differs from the slug. But by the concession of the materialist, we are not the same kind of beasts; and this we may also say from our own consciousness. Therefore, I think it must be the possession of a soul within us that makes the difference."

The clearest definition of the soul is found in Luke's rendering of the great question of Jesus. In Matthew and Mark it reads, "What shall it profit a man if he shall gain the whole world and lose his own soul?" (Matt. 16:26; Mark 8:36), but in Luke 9:25 it says, "What is a man advantaged, if he gain the whole world and lose himself, or be cast away?" This, then, is the soul. It is the person himself or herself. And as

Peter Marshall observed, "We are not bodies with souls, rather we are souls within bodies."

The old slave preachers used to tell a story about the time when the four spirits—earth, water, air, and fire—conspired to hide man's soul. They hid it in the earth, but man found it there. They hid it in the fire, but man found it there. They hid it in the air, but man found it there. They hid it in the water, but man found it there. Finally, in desperation they went to their master Satan and explained their dilemma. He heard their story and gave a scathing reply, "You fools! Did you think that you could hide man's soul in the earth, the fire, the air, or the water? I'll tell you where to hide man's soul. Hide it within himself. He'll never find it there." And so it is. The best that we are and the worst that we are is hidden deep within ourselves.

So then, honor your soul. Satan honors it, for he desires to have it. Christ honors it, for He shed his precious blood to redeem it. Angels honor it, for they rejoice over its salvation. Will you, too, honor your soul? Have you committed your soul to its faithful Redeemer? Are you living as an immortal soul created in the image of God? Is it well with your soul? Will you say today and every day from the depths of your being, "Bless the Lord, O my soul, and all that is within me. Bless His holy name" (Psalm 103:1)?

THE CLAIMS OF CHRIST

I and the Father are one.

—John 10:30 NIV

When I was a junior in college back in Iowa, I once attended an Intervarsity Christian Fellowship Conference at a Bible camp in Story City, Iowa. Students from colleges and universities all over the state came to hear an address on the Lordship of Christ by Dr. W. Robert Smith, chairman of the Department of Philosophy at the University of Dubuque. During the course of his sermon, Dr. Smith made a statement that completely changed my thinking about our Lord Jesus Christ and, as a matter of fact, changed my entire life. I am quite sure that I would not be speaking as a minister of the gospel had I not heard that statement. What Dr. Smith said was simply this: "Either Jesus Christ is what He claimed to be or He is the world's greatest imposter."

I had never thought of it quite that way before. If Jesus Christ is not what He claimed to be, then He is the biggest liar who ever lived. Because, you see, He made a greater claim than any person who has ever lived. He claimed to be God.

The classic work on the divinity of Christ is a work entitled *The Divinity of Our Lord* by H. P. Liddon. The book is based on eight lectures delivered by Canon Liddon on that subject at Oxford University in 1867. Although Rev. Liddon was a substitute for the original lecturer and prepared the series on very short notice, the book has been a standard for over one hundred years. In the lectures he marshals the evidence in Scripture and church history that affirms the deity of Christ. One of the chapters has to do with what Christ Himself claimed. Liddon points out three things that are Christ's claims to divinity. He claimed to be equal with the Father. He claimed to be one with the Father. And He claimed pre-existence with the Father.

C. S. Lewis, late professor of Renaissance Literature at Oxford and Cambridge, was one who discovered this. Even after his conversion, he did not believe that Jesus Christ was the Son of God. But somehow he came to believe. He simply said that he left Oxford on his motorcycle not believing that Jesus Christ was the Son of God and arrived at the Whipsnade Zoo believing that he was. It was the end of a long journey.

C. S. Lewis has this to say to those who are willing to accept Jesus as a great teacher but not as the Son of God. He says, "That is the one thing that we must not say. For how can we accept Jesus as a great teacher if we do not accept what he taught about himself?"

BEHOLDING JESUS

Then came Jesus forth, wearing the crown of thorns, and the purple robe. And Pilate saith unto them, "Behold the man!"

—John 19:5

And what a man! No man was ever born like Jesus. No man ever lived like Jesus. No man ever worked like Jesus. No man ever taught like Jesus. No man ever died like Jesus. No man ever rose again like Jesus. He is the central character of the centuries, for all time is divided by His birth—before Christ and in the year of our Lord. All the armies that ever marched, all the navies that ever sailed, all the parliaments that ever sat have not had as much effect upon the human race as has this one perfect life. He is the subject of the world's greatest book, the Holy Bible. He is the subject of the world's greatest painting—Leonardo Da Vinci's "Last Supper." He is the subject of the world's greatest piece of music—Handel's *Messiah*. He is the most unique person who ever lived.

There is nothing that reveals the greatness of the man Christ Jesus more than the various titles given Him in the Bible. Let me list just some of those. He is called the Almighty, Alpha and Omega, Arm of the Lord, Author and Finisher of Our Faith, Author of Eternal Salvation, Blessed and Only Potentate, Chief Shepherd, Cornerstone, Counselor, Creator, Deliverer, Desire of All Nations, Everlasting, Father, Glory of the Lord, God, Governor, Head of the Church, Heir of All Things, Holy One of God, Image of God, King of the Ages, King of Kings, Lamb of God, Life, Light of the World, Lord of All, Lord of Lords, Lord Our Righteousness, Mighty God, Our Passover, Prince of Peace, Resurrection and the Life, Son of God, Truth, Word of God. No other person who has lived has had such words applied to him. Behold the man!

Dear friend, have you beheld Him? Have you beheld Jesus Christ? Have you beheld the tiny baby lying in a manger, the glory as of the only begotten of the Father full of grace and truth? Have you beheld Him as He healed the sick, gave sight to the blind, and raised the dead? Have you beheld Him hanging in agony and shame upon the cross, dying for you and for me? Have you beheld Him as He burst forth from the tomb on the third day triumphant over sin and death and hell and the grave? Have you beheld Him standing at the right hand of the throne of God making intercession for us? Behold Him. Behold the man. Behold His cross. Behold your King.

KEEP LOOKING UP

Wherefore seeing we also are compassed about with so great a cloud of witnesses, let us lay aside every weight, and the sin which doth so easily beset us, and let us run with patience the race that is set before us. Looking unto Jesus the author and finisher of our faith; who for the joy that was set before him endured the cross, despising the shame, and is set down at the right hand of the throne of God.

—Hebrews 12:1-2

The first two verses of Hebrews 12 not only exhort us to keep looking up, but they also tell us how to do that. So, then, keep looking up to the saints in glory. The expression "cloud of witnesses" in verse 1 is a reference to the heroes of the faith whose names are listed in the previous chapter: Noah, Abraham, Joseph, Moses, and many others. Hebrews 11 is the faith chapter of the Bible, for these people are offered to us as examples of what faith can do in a human life. Then keep looking up to the highest and noblest Christian virtues. "Let us lay aside every weight and the sin which doth so easily beset us, and let us run with patience the race that is set before us" (Heb. 12:1b).

Many people become discouraged in the Christian life because they think that when they become Christians everything should be perfect, including themselves. It doesn't work that way. That's what Paul meant when he said, "I count not myself to have apprehended" (Phil. 3:13a). A Christian is not one who is perfect, but a Christian is one who wants to be perfect. Please be patient; God isn't finished with you yet.

And finally, keep looking up to Jesus, the Author and Finisher of our faith. "Looking unto Jesus, the Author and Finisher of our Faith, who for the joy that was set before him, endured the cross, despising the shame, and is set down at the right hand of the throne of God." Wherever else we look for help and encouragement in our spiritual journey we must ultimately look to Jesus. Like the disciples—Peter,

James, and John—on the Mount of Transfiguration, the vision of other helpers must fade and we must see no man save Jesus only.

He is not only the author of our faith. He is also the finisher of our faith. That means that God never gives up on us. The apostle Paul reminded his young friend Timothy, "He who has begun a good work in you will perform it unto the day of Jesus Christ" (Phil. 1:6). As one little boy put it in a poster, "God don't make no junk." God did not choose you to fail or to fall. No matter what you experience in life, no matter how many trials and temptations come your way, God has promised to see you through. As the apostle Paul said, "I reckon that the sufferings of this present time are not worthy to be compared with the glory that will be revealed in us" (Rom. 8:18). Keep looking up to Jesus, the Author and Finisher of your faith.

FOLLOWERS OF GOD

Be ye therefore followers of God as dear children. And walk in love, as Christ also has loved us and hath given Himself for us, an offering and a sacrifice to God for a sweet-smelling savour.

—Ephesians 5:1-2

In Ephesians 5:l we read these words, "Be ye therefore followers of God, as dear children." These words serve to remind us that as the children of God we are the followers of God. For Jesus said, "I am the light of the world, he that followeth me shall not walk in darkness but shall have the light of life" (John 8:12). And again, "If any man would come after me let him deny himself and take up his cross daily and follow me" (Matt. 16:24). And, "He that forsaketh not all that he hath and followeth me cannot be my disciple" (Luke 14:33). The children of God are intended to be followers of God.

When we turn to the Revised Standard Version of the New Testament we find, I think, a more accurate translation of these words and a better indication of the type of character expected of the children of God. In this case we read, "Therefore be imitators of God, as beloved children." The Greek word which is translated "followers" in the one case and "imitators" in the other is the word *mimatas* from which we derive our English words "mimic" and "imitate." You see, then, as God's children we are to mimic God. We are to imitate God in character and conduct. We are to be imitators of God.

I suppose that there is no man who lived a more godly life than John Wesley, the founder of Methodism. He preached for sixty years and delivered over forty thousand sermons. He rode ten thousand miles every year on horseback. He suffered with tuberculosis. He often faced hostile mobs but conquered them with kindness. All who knew him agreed, this man walked with God. I think that the key to John Wesley's life are words which appear on the first page of his famous diary. Would to God that these words might direct your life and mine. Mr. Wesley wrote: "A general rule in all actions of life whenever you are to do an action, consider how God did or would do the like, and do you imitate His example."

> Earthly pleasures vainly call me, I would be like Jesus;
> Nothing worldly shall enthrall me, I would be like Jesus.
>
> All the way from earth to glory, I would be like Jesus;
> Telling o'er and o'er the story, I would be like Jesus.
>
> Be like Jesus, this my song, in the home and in the throng;
> Be like Jesus, all day long! I would be like Jesus.
>
> (James Rowe, "I Would Be Like Jesus")

THE RESURRECTION
AND THE LIFE

Jesus said to her, "I am the resurrection and the life. He who believes in Me, though he may die, he shall live. And whoever lives and believes in Me will never die."

—John 11:25-26a NKJV

This verse in John 11:25 is, of course, one of the seven "I am" sayings in John's Gospel. Like the others, it contains a claim, a promise, and a condition. The claim is "I am the resurrection and the life." The promise is "though he may die, he shall live and will never die." The condition is "believes."

Actually, there are two claims here. Jesus is really saying "I am the resurrection" and "I am the life." It is just as in John 14:6 where He says, "I am the Way, the Truth and the Life." He is making three claims: "I am the Way," "I am the Truth," and "I am the Life." Thomas a Kempis said of those words, "Without the Way there is no going, without the Truth there is no knowing and without the Life there is no living." So here we might say, Without Christ, who is the resurrection, there is no rising from the dead; and without Christ, who is the life, there is no life after death. As the Apostle's Creed states, "I believe in the resurrection of the body and the life everlasting."

When I think of Jesus' words "I am the resurrection and the life," I am reminded of a scene from Charles Dickens' great novel *A Tale of Two Cities*. Perhaps you remember the plot. Sydney Carton, the hero of the story, is in love with a woman who does not love him, but instead loves a man who bears a striking resemblance to Carton. It was during the French Revolution. This man, the woman's true love, was arrested and sentenced to die on the guillotine. Sydney Carton went to Paris to secure the release of the man but was unsuccessful. Then, a strange idea came to him. He realized, because of his close resemblance to the prisoner, that he could enter the prison and trade places with this other

181

man and die on the guillotine in order that the woman he loved might have her true love. As he walked the streets of Paris struggling with this plan, a verse of Scripture flashed into his mind. It seemed that his very footsteps beat out the rhythm of those words on the cobblestones as he walked: "I am the resurrection and the life." "I am the resurrection and the life." "I am the resurrection and the life." It was then that he decided to follow through with his plan. As he walked to the guillotine to die in another man's place for the woman he loved, he said to himself, "It is a far better thing that I do than I have ever done before." And any person who takes up his cross to follow Jesus Christ can say, "It is a far better thing that I do than I have ever done before."

THE RESURRECTION OF THE BODY

We will not all sleep, but we will all be changed—in a flash, in the twinkling of an eye, at the last trumpet. For the trumpet will sound, the dead will be raised imperishable, and we will be changed.
—1 Corinthians 15:51b-52 NIV

"I believe in the resurrection of the body and the life everlasting." So reads the Apostle's Creed, the one creed to which Christians of all faiths subscribe. And this is the subject of 1 Corinthians 15, known as the resurrection chapter of the Bible.

This letter was written by Paul to the Christians in Corinth to correct certain errors of faith and life that existed within that church. He writes regarding the various factions into which the church is divided. He writes about the work of the minister. He writes about immorality within the church. He writes about Christian marriage, about the abuse of the Lord's Supper, and the misuse of spiritual gifts. And then, in chapter 15 he deals with what he must have considered the most grievous fault of the church—the denial on the part of some of its members, at least, of the resurrection of the body. Paul asks, "How say some among you that there is no resurrection of the dead?" (v. 12b).

Now, it will help us to understand this problem if we can remember that the people to whom Paul addressed this portion of his letter were most likely Gentiles and Greeks. They did not have the advantage of a Jewish religious background, for all Jewish religious sects, with the exception of the Sadducees, believe in the resurrection of the body. In the pagan world the situation was just the opposite. All of the Greek religions and philosophies, with the exception of some of the mystery religions, taught that only the spirit survives death. This aspect of Greek thought had been carried over into the Corinthian church, or at least some elements of it. And it is to correct this error that Paul writes this chapter.

A few years ago Sylvia and I had the privilege of visiting the village of Epworth in England. Epworth is famous as the birthplace of John and Charles Wesley, the founders of Methodism. Charles was the hymn writer and John the preacher. We visited the Wesley home where Samuel and Sarah Wesley reared their nineteen children and where John and Charles lived until they left to attend Oxford University. Years later, when John had begun the great revival movement that swept England under his leadership, he returned to Epworth and asked permission to preach in the church where his father had served as pastor for over forty years. The new vicar refused and so John stood outside the church following the service on Sunday and asked people to come back and hear him preach in the cemetery that afternoon. A great crowd of people gathered in the cemetery that was adjacent to the church, and Wesley stood on his father's tombstone and preached on the words of St. Paul: "The kingdom of God is not meat and drink, but righteousness and peace and joy in the Holy Ghost" (Rom. 14:17). And so, dear friend, today as the church has through the centuries, we stand on the ground of the empty tomb of the living Christ and offer to humankind the hope and promise of the resurrection of the body and the life everlasting.

A LESSON FROM THE GEESE

Encourage the timid, help the weak, be patient with everyone.
—1 Thessalonians 5:14b NIV

Mark Twain once said, "I could live for a whole month on one good compliment." Giving a deserved compliment is one way we can encourage another person. There are many other ways to be an encourager. As we look forward to spring, we are encouraged when we see the first robin or hear the honking of the geese as they fly over. Perhaps we could learn a lesson or two about encouragement from the geese.

Do you know why geese fly in formation? They are encouraging one another! When the lead goose gets tired, another one takes its place. Flying as they do, each goose creates an upward air current for the one behind. The whole flock gets 71 percent greater wing power than if each bird flew alone. When one goose is sick or wounded, two fall out of their formation to follow it down and protect it. They stay with the struggler until it is able to fly again. The geese in the rear of the formation are the ones who do the honking. It's their way of encouraging those in front to stay at it.

Whether it's leading, flapping, helping, or simply honking, the flock is in it together. Thus, the teamwork enables them to reach their destination. We all have the opportunity to build endurance in one another when it's needed. We can support each other in prayer. Be cheerful and positive when things go wrong. Avoid criticism. Give praise freely. Be quick to give a helping hand.

In His Word, God has commanded us to be encouragers. You will grow spiritually; others will be challenged to keep on, and we can be a witness for Jesus by the way we live. "Therefore encourage one another and build each other up, just as in fact you are doing" (1 Thess. 5:11 NIV). "Let us encourage one another—and all the more as you see the Day approaching" (Heb. 10:25b NIV).

185

THE NEW BIRTH

In reply Jesus declared, "I tell you the truth, no one can see the kingdom of God unless he is born again."

—John 3:3 NIV

In the seventeenth century there lived in Bedford, England, a young man who was a tinker by trade. One summer day he sat on the back steps of a cottage repairing the pots and pans of the family that lived there. As he did so, he heard through the hedge that separated two houses the strangest conversation in his life. For next door two women were talking about an experience which they called the new birth. This young man had never heard that expression before, and his curiosity was aroused. He soon realized that they were talking about something which was described in the Bible. So this young man began to read the Bible with the result that he experienced the new birth. His life was changed and the lives of millions of others were changed also. For the young man's name was John Bunyan, whom we remember as the author of *Pilgrim's Progress*. It has been said that this Christian classic has been read by more people in the world than any other book with the single exception of the Holy Bible. I think that it might even be possible to say that *Pilgrim's Progress* has had more influence in the world than any other book except the Holy Bible. And it all began when a young tinker heard a conversation between two women about the new birth. Such is the miracle of the new birth.

You have, no doubt, been hearing and reading a great deal about the term "born again" in recent years. It all began with the conversion of Chuck Colson, President Nixon's attorney. After his indictment in the Watergate affair, Colson turned to Christ and while in prison wrote his story in a book entitled *Born Again*. Chuck Colson's experience should convince anyone that there is such a thing as the miracle of the new birth. However, please understand that you do not have to go to prison to be born again. To be born again is not the experience of only a few super saints. It is the normal Christian experience. To be a Christian is to be born again. To be born again is to be a Christian.

And what does one need to do to be born again? The answer is quite simple. Believe on the Lord Jesus Christ and receive Him who died on the cross for you as your Savior. "To all who received Him, to those who believed in His name, He gave the right to become children of God" (John 1:12 NIV).

In his great crusades, millions of people have joined Billy Graham as he has led them in prayer and have been born again as they have prayed: "I know that I am a sinner and need Your forgiveness. I believe that You died for my sins. I want to turn from my sins. I now invite You to come into my heart and life. I want to trust and follow You as Lord and Savior. In Jesus' name. Amen."

THE JOY OF THE CROSS

Let us fix our eyes on Jesus, the author and perfecter of our faith, who for the joy set before Him endured the cross, scorning its shame, and sat down at the right hand of the throne of God.

—Hebrews 12:2 NIV

In Hebrews 12:2 we find these words: "Looking unto Jesus, the author and finisher of our faith; who for the joy that was set before him endured the cross." In John 15 and 16, Jesus is gathered in the upper room with His disciples. He knows that He is going to die and is preparing His disciples for His death. Nevertheless, in those two chapters He speaks no less than six times of His joy. In John 17 we have the record of the prayer which our Lord offered in the Garden of Gethsemane. Even there He prayed for His disciples that "they might have my joy fulfilled in themselves" (v. 13). The apostle Paul, speaking of the possibility of his martyrdom, says, "If I be offered...I joy and rejoice" (Phil. 2:17).

Mrs. Peter Marshall, who has known what it is to bear her cross (she had tuberculosis), tells a very interesting parable in a little book for children called *Friends with God*. The story is about a king who commissioned the artists of the land to paint a picture of their conception of peace. A wonderful prize was to be offered for the best picture. After looking at all the pictures there were two that the king thought best and he attempted to choose between them. The one was a picture filled with sunshine and flowers. The other was a picture of a barren mountain in the midst of a severe thunderstorm. And which picture did the king choose? The picture of sunshine? No, he chose the picture of the thunderstorm. For in that picture, almost unobservable, could be seen a mother bird sitting upon her nest in the cleft of a rock safe from the storm. "This," said the king, "is the perfect picture of peace."

189

Let us therefore walk with patience the path that is set before us, the path through our Gethsemane and to our Calvary, looking unto Jesus, the author and finisher of our faith, who for the joy that was set before him endured the cross.

THE FULLNESS OF THE SPIRIT

Be filled with the Spirit.

—Ephesians 5:18b

A number of years ago Billy Graham and his wife spent a brief vacation in Switzerland as the guests of Karl Barth, the noted Swiss theologian. During the course of their conversations, Dr. Graham asked his host what he thought would be the next emphasis in theology. Dr. Barth replied without hesitation, "The Holy Spirit."

Before he died, Pope John Paul was asked what church doctrine most needed emphasis today. He replied, "The doctrine of the Holy Spirit."

As we read the book of Acts and compare the church in the first century with the church in America in the twenty-first century, we soon come to realize that the difference is due to the place that the Holy Spirit played in the lives of those first Christians. And we can only pray with Isaac Watts,

Come, Holy Spirit, Heavenly Dove, with all thy quickening powers;
Kindle a flame of sacred love in these cold hearts of ours.

The verb "fill" as it is used here has nothing to do with content or quantity, as though we are empty vessels that need a required amount of spiritual fuel to keep going. In the Bible, filled often means, as it does here, "controlled by." For example, we are told in the gospels that when Jesus preached in the synagogue in Nazareth that "all in the synagogue were filled with wrath" and tried to kill him. That means that they were controlled by wrath. In the book of Acts we are told that the Jews opposed the ministry of Paul and Barnabas because they were "filled with envy." That means that they were controlled by envy. To be "filled with the Spirit" means to be constantly controlled by the Spirit in our minds, our emotions, and our will.

How does one become filled with the Holy Spirit? This expression is literally translated "filled in Spirit." That expression occurs three other times in Ephesians—in Ephesians 2:22, with regard to the church; in 3:5, with regard to the Bible; and in 6:18, with regard to the prayer life of the Christian. With the help of the church, the Bible, and prayer we are enabled to turn from sin and turn to Christ and so be filled with the holy Spirit.

I am convinced that to be filled with the Spirit is not an option, but a necessity. It is indispensable for the abundant life and for fruitful service. The Spirit-filled life is not abnormal; it is the normal Christian life. Anything less is subnormal; it is less than what God wants and provides for His children. Therefore, to be filled with the Spirit should never be thought of as an unusual or unique experience for, or known by, only a select few. It is intended for all, needed by all, and available to all. That is why the Scripture commands all of us, "Be filled with the Spirit."

BLOOD AND TEARS

Blessed are those who are persecuted because of righteousness, for theirs is the kingdom of heaven.

—Matthew 5:10 NIV

"I have nothing to offer but blood, toil, tears, and sweat." These words were spoken by Winston Churchill in the House of Commons on May 10, 1940, when he became Prime Minister of Great Britain in the darkest hour of World War II. On any other occasion these words would seem melodramatic in an inaugural address, but on this occasion, the military situation made them entirely appropriate.

The Sermon on the Mount is, of course, Jesus' inaugural address. At the very beginning he speaks words not unlike those of Churchill: "Blessed are those that are persecuted for righteousness sake; for theirs is the Kingdom of Heaven." These words are appropriate here because Jesus foresaw the opposition of the Roman authorities and the Jewish religious leaders. In fact, He spoke to people of all time when He said, "If any man would come after me, let him deny himself and take up his cross daily and follow me" (Luke 9:23).

This Beatitude is a relevant statement for people in every country at this moment. There are so many indications that the church may indeed be facing the greatest period of persecution in its history. We have no reason to believe that Americans, living now in apparent safety and ease, will always be exempt from such things. We must remember the words of the apostle Paul, "All they that will live godly in Christ Jesus shall suffer persecution" (2 Tim. 3:12). Let us be clear, then, that we understand this verse and know exactly what it does say.

Let us ask ourselves this question: Do we know what it is to be persecuted for righteousness' sake? We are not to be offensive; we are not to be foolish; we are not to be unwise; we are not even to parade the Christian faith. We are not to do anything that calls for persecution.

But by just being like Christ, persecution becomes inevitable. If you find yourself persecuted for righteousness' sake, you have in a sense got the final proof of the fact that you are a Christian, that you are a citizen of the kingdom of Heaven. As Paul says, "For unto you it is given in behalf of Christ, not only to believe on Him, but also to suffer for His sake" (Phil. 1:29).

May God through His Holy Spirit give us great wisdom, discrimination, knowledge, and understanding in these things, so that if ever we are called upon to suffer, we may know for certain that it is for righteousness' sake and may have the full comfort and consolation of this glorious Beatitude.

REST IN THE LORD

For we who have believed do enter that rest.

—Hebrews 4:3a NKJV

On one occasion I went on a shopping tour with my three sons to buy something nice for their mother. It was not an easy decision. After I talked them out of a new catcher's mitt and several things like that, we agreed that flowers would be nice for Mother. Off to the flower shop we went. And then came the decision as to what kind of flowers to buy. As we were browsing through the shop the boys called from a corner, "Come here, Dad. This would be nice for Mom." They had found a very lovely bouquet indeed. However, it was not quite suitable. For on the bouquet was a ribbon and on the ribbon the words "Rest in Peace." This is not the kind of present that one gives to a living mother.

We chuckle at this because we have reserved the words "Rest in Peace" for those who are dead. But I wonder if this is proper. Can only the dead find rest and peace? As a matter of fact, we find that we have even perverted the Scripture in this regard. For on many tombstones we find a paraphrase of the words of Hebrews 4:3—"Entered into rest on such and such a day," signifying the date of the person's death. But the words of Hebrew 4:3 do not say that we shall have rest only when we die. They read, "For we which have believed do enter into rest." Not *shall* enter into rest but *do* enter into rest. Spiritual rest ought therefore to be the present possession of every Christian as well as his or her future hope.

Now I would not want to minimize in any way the importance of heavenly rest. For the Scriptures declare, "Blessed are the dead who die in the Lord...for they rest from their labors and their works do follow them" (Rev. 14:13). And the first definition that the dictionary gives of *rest* is this: "to get repose by lying down; esp. to sleep: also to be dead."

I would certainly emphasize, therefore, the importance of life's first question, "Quo Vadis? Where goest thou?" For no man can hope to have earthly rest in the highest sense of that word who has not already assured himself of that heavenly rest.

And there are other meanings of this word that apply to the Christian gospel. To rest means "to cease from action or motion; to desist from exertion; to be still." Some of us who may be reading this today have that as the greatest need of our lives; to stop struggling with ourselves and with God. "Be still; and know that I am God" (Psalm 46:10).

The word also means to lie, "to be fixed or supported; as a column rests on a pedestal." Jesus Christ is our Cornerstone. And so it is that our faith is fixed on Jesus Christ. Our faith rests on Jesus Christ. "Upon a life I did not live; upon a death I did not die: upon another's life, another's death, I rest my whole eternity."

And a fourth definition of that word *rest* means "to repose without anxiety; to trust, to rely, to depend." And here is a sermon in itself. Our churches are filled with anxious Christians who have trusted God for eternity but not for today.

This ought not to be. And if it is true in our lives it is because we have not trusted Christ enough. We have enough faith to believe that we shall rest in death, but not enough to believe that we can rest in life. We need more faith. "Why are you fearful, O you of little faith?" (Matt. 8:26 NKJV).

SOLDIERS OF GOD

Put on the full armor of God so that you can take your stand against the devil's schemes.

—Ephesians 6:11 NIV

One thing that has always been of great interest to me as I have read the various letters of Paul in the New Testament is the apostle's unusual interest in military matters. I say unusual because if you will remember that Paul was often the prisoner of the Roman government and, therefore, often guarded by Roman soldiers, one would think that if there is any part of his life that he would want to obliterate from his consciousness, it would be the part that has to do with things military.

Quite the opposite is true. There are references in nearly all of Paul's letters to military life. As a matter of fact, he even goes so far as to suggest that his friends in those little churches that he founded throughout the empire might very well exemplify in their lives some of the sterling qualities of those noble Roman legionnaires. For example, he writes to his young friend Timothy, "Thou, therefore, endure hardness as a good soldier of Jesus Christ"(2 Tim. 2:3). In another place he says, "Fight the good fight of faith" (1 Tim. 6:12). In the last letter that he wrote, Paul summarizes his own matchless life and ministry with a military metaphor: "I have fought a good fight; I have finished my course; I have kept the faith" (2 Tim. 4:7). But of all the passages in the New Testament there is none greater than the clarion call to arms that we have in these words, "Put on the whole armor of God" (Eph. 6:11).

Now, as we think of these things, the question that begs to be answered is: What is it that Paul saw in these Roman legionnaires that he felt should be part and parcel of every genuine Christian's makeup? What is it, after all, that soldiers and saints have in common?

When General Robert E. Lee, who was both a soldier and a saint, enrolled his son in the military academy at West Point, his parting words to him were, "Duty is the most sublime word in the language. You can never do more; you should never want to do less."

It is this deep sense of commitment that characterizes both soldier and saint. To be a good soldier means to be completely committed to one's cause and one's commander. To be a good soldier of Jesus Christ means to be completely committed to Him and His cause in the world.

> Rise up, O children of God!
> Have done with lesser things:
> Give heart and soul and mind and strength
> To serve the King of Kings.
> (William P. Merrill, "Rise Up, O Men of God")

A MATTER OF LIFE AND DEATH

For to me, to live is Christ and to die is gain.

—Philippians 1:21 NIV

In an interview on Larry King's show, Billy Graham was asked the question, "Aren't you afraid to die?"

Mr. Graham replied, "Oh no, I want to die because then I will be with Christ."

As you know, God has not chosen to grant Dr. Graham's desire, so he continues preaching. As a matter of fact, he said on that same show, "People in the Bible never retired."

Although some might see that as a no-win situation, Paul sees it as a win-win situation, for he says, "For me to live is Christ and to die is gain." That was the motto of Paul's life and the creed by which he lived. The same should be said of every Christian.

What did Paul mean when he said, "For to me to live is Christ"? The writers of the New Testament teach us that there is no life apart from Christ. Life is a key word in the Gospel of John. As John describes the origin of the creation in the first chapter of his gospel, he says of Christ, "In Him was life and the life was the light of men" (v. 4). In John 11, just before Jesus raises His friend Lazarus from the dead, He says, "I am the resurrection and the life; he that believes in me, though he was dead, yet shall he live and whoever lives and believes in me shall never die" (v. 25). In John 14, in a conversation with the apostles just before he went to the cross, Jesus says, "I am the Way, the Truth and the Life" (v. 6). John 3:36 says: "He who believes in the Son has everlasting life; and he who does not believe the Son shall not see life, but the wrath of God abides on him" (NKJV). It is only when we believe on Christ that we have life. Jesus says, "I tell you the truth, whoever hears my word and believes Him who sent me has eternal life and will not be condemned; he has crossed over from death to life" (John 5:24).

LIKE FATHER, LIKE SON

Dear friends, now we are children of God, and what we will be has not yet been made known. But we know that when He appears, we shall be like Him, for we shall see Him as He is.

—1 John 3:2 NIV

March 28, 1951 was an important date in the life of Sylvia and myself. For on that day our first child was born. As I went about my usual activities in the next few days—classes at seminary and my job at the insurance company—everyone asked the same question: "Who does he look like?" It took me a few days to realize that, as a matter of fact, he looked like me. Come to think of it, I look like my father and he looked like his father. That's the way that it is supposed to be. Like father, like son.

As you know, preachers are always looking for analogies between earthly and heavenly things. So I asked myself, "Is it also true that the sons of God should be like their heavenly Father?" Then I remembered these words from 1 John 3:2, "Beloved, now are we the sons of God and it does not yet appear what we shall be, but we know that when He shall appear that we shall be like Him." What a great promise that is! Every promise in the Bible carries with it a responsibility. As Paul says to the Ephesians, "Be imitators of God, therefore, as dearly loved children and live a life of love, just as Christ loved us" (5:1-2 NIV). *We have His name.* "See how much the Father has loved us! His love is so great that we are called God's children—and so, in fact, we are" (1 John 3:1 TEV).

We find also that *we shall resemble the Father in His appearance.* In verse 2 John declares, "Beloved now are we the children of God and it does not yet appear what we shall be; but we know that when He shall appear we shall be like Him." We shall resemble the Father, for when Jesus comes we will be like Him and Jesus said, "He who has seen Me has seen the Father" (John 14:9b NKJV).

Not only do we resemble our heavenly Father in His name and in His appearance but *we resemble Him most important of all in His character*. In verse 9 John writes, "No one who is born of God will continue to sin, because God's seed remains in him; he cannot go on sinning, because he has been born of God" (NIV).

A man visited the office of President Lincoln one day, and when he had gone Mr. Lincoln said, "I didn't like that man."

His secretary was startled to hear the kindly Mr. Lincoln say such a thing. He said, "Mr. President, what was it that you didn't like about him?" Mr. Lincoln said, "I didn't like his face."

"But, Mr. President," the secretary remonstrated, "the man is not responsible for his face. He was born with it." Lincoln replied, "A man may not be responsible for his face before the age of forty, but after that he is." And I tell you a man may not be responsible for his face before he is a Christian but after that he is. No man who has lost the weight of sin has a right to look as if he carried the weight of the world on his shoulder. No man who sings "What a Friend We Have in Jesus" has a right to look as if he had lost his last friend.

THE LIFE OF FAITH
IN THE AGE OF ANXIETY

Lord, you have been our dwelling place throughout all generations.
—Psalm 90:1 NIV

The time in which we live has been described as "The Age of Anxiety." There is plenty of evidence for believing that. It is indicated by the incredible amounts of tranquilizing drugs, the tons of sleeping pills, and the billions of dollars worth of alcoholic beverages consumed by Americans each year. It is indicated by the emergence of heart attacks as a leading cause of death in our society, by the marked increase in suicide among our youth, and by the alarming increase in crimes of violence in our country.

Dr. Paul Tillich, professor of theology at Harvard University, in his best-selling masterpiece *The Courage to Be,* identifies three primary sources of anxiety in contemporary life. First, there is the anxiety of death and non-being. Then, there is the anxiety of guilt and condemnation. And finally, the anxiety of emptiness and meaninglessness. According to Tillich every form of anxiety fits one of these three categories. I think that our own experience testifies to the accuracy of Tillich's analysis.

One day as I was reading Psalm 90, a prayer of Moses, the man of God, I was struck by the fact that the great prophet deals with these three forms of anxiety in his plaintive song. In verses 1 through 6, he expresses the anxiety of death and non-being as he elaborates on the frailty of man and the brevity of life: "Thou carriest them away as with a flood; they are as a sleep; in the morning they are like grass which groweth up. In the morning it flourisheth and groweth up; in the evening it is cut down and withereth" (vv. 5-6). In verses 7 through 12 there is expressed the anxiety of guilt and condemnation, for Moses explains death as punishment for sin: "For we are consumed by thine anger, and by thy wrath are we troubled" (v. 11). Verses 13 through 17 are a prayer that God will honor the lives of His servants: "Establish thou the work of our hands upon us; yea, the work of our hands establish thou it" (v. 17). There is the anxiety of meaninglessness and emptiness.

But Psalm 90 is no mere dirge of death. For, like the canvas of an old Dutch master, it contains not only the deep, dark shadows which are a part of life, but also the soft light from heaven which gives meaning to it all. The Psalm begins with this mighty affirmation of faith: "Lord, thou hast been our dwelling place in all generations." There is the answer to anxiety. God is our dwelling place. Acts 17:28 tells us, "In Him we live and move and have our being." And Paul says, "Your life is hid with Christ in God" (Col. 3:3). This, then, is the life of faith in the age of anxiety: abide in Christ.

FAITH OF OUR FOUNDING FATHERS

Blessed is the nation whose God is the LORD, the people he chose for His inheritance.

—Psalm 33:12 NIV

Each year as we celebrate the birth of our nation, the ever-recurring question arises: Was the United States of America founded upon Christian principles? There are those who would argue that since the Declaration of Independence was produced by men whose views did not represent orthodox Christianity that, therefore, the document which they produced and the nation which they founded could not be Christian.

There was, however, one orthodox Christian on the five-man committee that was appointed to formulate the Declaration of Independence. Roger Sherman, a delegate to the Continental Congress from Connecticut, was a Puritan. He later served in the United States House of Representatives and also in the Senate. John Adams described him as "one of the most sensible men in the world." Jefferson said that Sherman was "a man who never said a foolish thing in his life."

Because the committee represented such diverse viewpoints, as did the Continental Congress as a whole, it could only be expected that the document which they produced would represent a compromise of their different positions. It would be well, then, to look at those statements in the Declaration that speak of God, bearing in mind that they may mean different things to different people. There are four such references.

The first sentence makes mention of God. "When in the course of human events, it becomes necessary for one people to dissolve the political bands which have connected them with another, and to assume among the powers of the earth, the separate and equal station to which the Laws of Nature and of *Nature's God* entitles them, a decent respect to the opinions of mankind requires that they should declare the causes which impel them to the separation."

The second sentence also speaks of God. "We hold these truths to be self-evident, that all men are created equal, that they are endowed by *their Creator* with certain unalienable rights, that among these are life, liberty and the pursuit of happiness."

The final paragraph of the document contains two more references to God. "We, therefore, the Representatives of the United States of America, in General Congress, assembled, appealing to the *Supreme Judge of the world* for the rectitude of our intentions, do, in the name, and by the Authority of the good People of these Colonies, solemnly publish and declare, that these United Colonies are, and of right ought to be free and independent states."

The final sentence of the Declaration of Independence reads, "And for the support of this Declaration, with a firm reliance on the protection of *divine Providence*, we mutually pledge to each other our lives, our fortunes and our sacred honor."

Creator. Judge. Protector. This is the theology of the Declaration of Independence. These are certainly ideas that are found in the Bible.

GOD'S PEACE CORPS

Blessed are the peacemakers: for they shall be called the children of God.
—Matthew 5:9

I believe that history will reveal that one of the most significant contributions of the administration of President John F. Kennedy was the establishment of the Peace Corps. The Peace Corps, as you may know, is an agency of the United States government that sends volunteers to instruct citizens of underdeveloped countries in industrial, agricultural, educational, and health programs. Sylvia and I had an opportunity to observe the work of the Peace Corps in Guatemala and Jamaica and can assure you that your tax dollars are being well invested by the Peace Corps. In fact, if we had more Peace Corps volunteers, we would not have to send military personnel to so many foreign places.

You know, God also has His Peace Corps. It was established by our Lord Jesus Christ in His final message to His disciples before His ascension. He said to His followers on that occasion, "Go ye into all the world and preach the gospel…" (Mark 16:15). His gospel is the gospel of peace. The Scripture says, "How beautiful are the feet of them that preach the gospel of peace" (Rom. 10:15). The benediction of Jesus upon God's Peace Corps is found in the seventh Beatitude: "Blessed are the peacemakers for they shall be called the children of God."

If you are a professing Christian you have been chosen to be a member of God's Peace Corps. For He needs businessmen, engineers, teachers, doctors, nurses, housewives, schoolchildren, and many others to bring this gospel of peace to the strife-torn world in which we live. By virtue of your Christian faith, you are a volunteer in God's Peace Corps.

Our first spiritual task as God's peacemakers is to enable people to make their peace with God. Paul says in the Epistle to the Romans,

"Therefore, being justified by faith, we have peace with God through our Lord Jesus Christ" (Rom. 5:1). And then, says Paul in his letter to the Philippians, "The peace of God which passes all understanding will keep your hearts and minds through Christ Jesus" (Phil. 4:7).

We are also to be peacemakers among people. The term *peacemaker* was used in the secular world in ancient times to describe an ambassador between nations. As Christians we are to be God's goodwill ambassadors in the world. We are to love our neighbor as our self and to teach others to do the same. A Christian should be a peacemaker in the home, at work, in school, in the church, in the community, and in the world.

GETTING IT ALL TOGETHER

If any of you lacks wisdom, he should ask God, who gives generously to all without finding fault, and it will be given to him.

—James 1:5 NIV

"Getting it all together" is an expression which we use today to indicate our desire to integrate all aspects of our lives into a meaningful whole. We want to maximize our efficiency and so enjoy life to the fullest.

Yes, we do want to get it all together. And be assured that God wants that for us as well. In this passage James says that for us as well. We are to be "perfect and complete, lacking in nothing" (James 1:4). And then he goes on to tell us how we can get it all together: "If any of you lacks wisdom, let him ask God, who gives to all men generously and without reproaching, and it will be given him" (1:5 RSV).

Note, then, for what we are to ask. In order to get it all together we are to ask for wisdom. Now most of us would not think first of wisdom as our greatest need in getting it all together. But you remember that Solomon, reputed to be the wisest man who ever lived, said, "Wisdom is the principal thing; therefore, get wisdom" (Prov. 4:7).

Then, note of whom we are to ask. We are to ask of God. "Let him ask God who gives to all men liberally." Most of us would be inclined to say that if you want more wisdom you should take a course at the university or read a book or get advice from some qualified counselor. But if we define wisdom, as I believe the Bible does, as the ability to see things from God's viewpoint, then it is to God Himself that we must go to obtain wisdom.

And, finally, note how we are to ask. It is through prayer, of course, that we ask of God. James talks about prayer again in the final chapter of this book and offers this great promise: "The prayer of a righteous man is powerful and effective" (James 5:16).

Getting it all together. Isn't that really what life is all about—finding meaning, purpose, and direction for our lives? Ultimately we do that only when we see life from God's viewpoint and live accordingly. That's why we pray in the Lord's Prayer, "Thy will be done on earth as it is in heaven" (Matt. 6:10b). God has already answered that prayer in the person of our Lord and Savior Jesus Christ. "In Him," says Paul, "are hidden all of the treasures of wisdom and knowledge" (Col. 2:3).

THE SMITTEN SERVANT

We all, like sheep, have gone astray, each of us has turned to his own way,
and the LORD has laid on Him the iniquity of us all.
                                                    —Isaiah 53:6 NIV

The fifty-third chapter of Isaiah is the Mt. Everest of Messianic prophecy. This portion of Isaiah's book, beginning at 52:13 and continuing to the end of chapter 53 consists of five servant poems. They speak of a smitten servant. And Christians recognize that servant as Jesus Christ. For when Isaiah says, "He was wounded for our transgressions, He was bruised for our iniquities: the chastisement of our peace was upon Him; and with His stripes we are healed" (53:5), we can almost see the cross of Calvary. And when Isaiah says, "He was oppressed, and He was afflicted, yet He opened not His mouth: He is brought as a lamb to the slaughter, and as a sheep before her shearers is dumb, so He opened not His mouth" (53:7), we see Him standing silent in the judgment hall of Pilate. When the prophet writes, "He made His grave with the wicked, and with the rich in His death"(53:9a), we remember that our Lord died between two thieves and that He was buried in the tomb of Joseph of Arimathea, a wealthy lawyer. And when Isaiah says that this servant made intercession for the transgressors, we are reminded that even on the cross our Savior prayed, "Father, forgive them" (Luke 23:34).

> Upon that cross of Jesus mine eye at times can see
> The very dying form of one who suffered there for me;
> And from my smitten heart with tears, two wonders I confess,
> The glory of redeeming love and my unworthiness.
>   (Elizabeth C. Clephane, "Beneath the Cross of Jesus")

And so it is that everyone who looks for a moment at that cross is changed for eternity. He becomes a smitten servant like the one upon the cross. For certainly every Christian must be a smitten servant.

Such a Christian was Dr. James Simpson, a famous British scientist. After his death friends who were examining his well-worn Bible noticed that he had changed all of the pronouns in Isaiah 53 to first-person pronouns: "He was wounded for *my* transgressions, He was bruised for *my* iniquities; the chastisement of *my* peace was upon Him; and with His stripes *I* was healed."

THE QUALITY OF MERCY

Blessed are the merciful, for they will be shown mercy.
—Matthew 5:7 NIV

If we are to learn how to show mercy we cannot look in the natural human heart, but must rather look to God. In the Old Testament the word *mercy* occurs more than 150 times, and on more than nine-tenths of the occasions the reference is to God and the actions of God. The same Hebrew word is sometimes translated "kindness," and it is kindness which is the basic idea of the word. Mercy is the outgoing kindness of the heart of God. It is the basis of God's whole relationship to man. One of the most oft-repeated statements in the Old Testament is that the mercy of God endures forever.

Since this mercy is the characteristic of God in his relationship with man, it is only to be expected that God wishes this mercy to be the characteristic of men's relationship with each other. The prophet Micah sums up the whole duty of man in the commandments "to do justice, and to love mercy and to walk humbly with thy God" (6:8b).

In the Old Testament mercy is no negative thing: it is not merely the agreement to suspend judgment or to remit penalty. It is the outgoing love of God to His people, a love to which God is pledged and to which He will be forever true, a love which is seen in the processes of nature and in the events of history, a love on which the whole relationship of man and God depends, an outgoing love which men must reproduce in their relationships with each other.

Outstanding among the houses of worship in Europe is the beautiful modern cathedral in Coventry, England. The most striking feature of this great house of worship is the fact that it is attached to the ruins of the original fourteenth-century church which was destroyed by German fire bombs in an air raid in 1940. At one end of the ruins is a

213

stone altar with the words, "Father, forgive" engraved upon it. The altar was erected by a group of young people from Germany who spent an entire summer on the project. I was deeply impressed by this symbol because I lived in Germany for a year following World War II and I had seen many German cities that were completely destroyed. That altar impressed upon me the fact it is only at the cross that we receive forgiveness—and it is only at the cross that we receive the power to forgive. "Blessed are the merciful for they shall obtain mercy" is a testimony to the mighty grace of God.

Do you need the mercy of God for forgiveness and cleansing of your sin? Do you need grace in order to forgive others? Is there unforgiven sin in your life? Is there someone whom you have never been able to forgive? Then you must come to the cross where the mercy of God is revealed fully for all to see. Whether it is for the forgiveness of your sin or the power to forgive others, you must come to the cross.

THE HOLY VISION

Blessed are the pure in heart; for they shall see God.

—Matthew 5:8

Our Lord is not saying that we must be perfect to come to God, but He is saying that when we come we should want to be perfect. It is this thought that Charles Wesley expressed so well in his hymn "O For a Heart to Praise My God."

O for a heart to praise my God:
A heart from sin set free,
A heart that always feels Thy blood,
So freely spilt for me.

A heart resigned, submissive, meek,
My great Redeemer's throne;
Where only Christ is heard to speak,
Where Jesus reigns alone.

A heart in every thought renewed,
And full of love divine,
Perfect and right and pure and good,
A copy, Lord, of thine.

How can we see God? Obviously we cannot see God with the physical eye, for the Bible says that God is a spirit, and as Jesus said to His disciples following His resurrection, "A spirit does not have flesh and bones as you see me have"(Luke 24:39b). I believe that our Lord meant something like this—as with all the other Beatitudes, the promise is partly filled here and now. In a sense there is a vision of God even while we are in this world. Christian people can see God in a sense that nobody else can. The Christian can see God in nature, whereas the unbeliever cannot. The Christian sees God in the events of history. There is a vision possible to the eye of faith that no one else has. But there is a seeing also in the sense of knowing Him, a sense of feeling He is near and enjoying His presence. It is said of Moses in book of Hebrews that "he endured as seeing Him who is invisible" (11:27b). That is a part of it, and that is something that is possible to us here and now. Imperfect as we are, we can claim that even now we are seeing God in that sense: we are "seeing Him who is invisible." Another way we see Him is in our own experience, in His gracious dealing with us. That is seeing God.

This was the experience of Alfred Lord Tennyson. When Tennyson was advanced in years, he asked his son, who was to be the executor of his estate, to see that the publishers, when they collected his poems and put them in a single volume, should put "Crossing the Bar" at the end of the book. Why Tennyson made such a request we are not told. But we remember that when he was once asked what was his dearest wish, he answered, "A clearer vision of God." It would, therefore, seem an appropriate climax that the last lines in his volume of collected poems should read:

And though from out this bourne of time and place
The flood should bear me far,
I hope to see my Pilot face to face
When I have crossed the bar.

ONE DAY AT A TIME

This is the day the Lord has made; let us rejoice and be glad in it.
—Psalm 118:24

Day by day and with each passing moment,
Strength I find to meet my trials here;
Trusting in my Father's wise bestowment,
I've no cause for worry or for fear.
He whose heart is kind beyond all measure,
Gives unto each day what He deems best.
Lovingly, it's part of pain and pleasure,
Mingling toil with peace and rest.
(Karolina Sandell-Berg, "the Fanny Crosby of Sweden")

How often we are told to live one day at a time. How do you live one day at a time? First, ***don't dwell on the past.*** Remember Lot's wife. After being granted reprieve from the destruction of Sodom and Gomorrah she looked back as she fled the cities and was turned into a pillar of salt. Dwelling on the past immobilizes anyone.

Second, ***don't count on the future.*** Jesus said, "Do not worry about tomorrow, for tomorrow will worry about itself. Each day has enough trouble of its own" (Matt. 6:34 NIV). Mark Twain wrote, "I've lived a long time and I've had many things worry me; most of which never happened."

Third, ***live for today.*** When St. Francis was asked what he would do if he knew that he was going to die today, he replied, "I'd go right on working in my garden."

When Eleanor Roosevelt was asked how she managed to remain calm in the face of the criticism and ridicule which she received as an activist First Lady, she answered, "I have no regrets for the past and no fear of the future."

Yesterday is history. The future is mystery. Today is a gift. That's why we call it the present!

THE FACE OF JESUS CHRIST

For God, who said, "Let light shine out of darkness," made His light shine in our hearts to give us the light of the knowledge of the glory of God in the face of Christ.

—2 Corinthians 4:6

What did Jesus look like? It is impossible from the Scriptural record to determine an answer to the question. There is no physical description of Jesus in the Gospels. The Scripture tells us absolutely nothing about the physical appearance of Jesus of Nazareth.

However, we do have a physical description of Jesus from early Christian history. Publius Lentulus, reporting to the Roman Senate, gave the world a description of the Savior that has been preserved verbatim and handed down to us through succeeding generations. He drew this word picture of the Messiah:

There appeared in those days a man of great virtue, named Jesus Christ, who is yet among us, of the Gentiles accepted as a prophet of truth, but His disciples call Him the Son of God.

He raises the dead, and cures all manner of diseases. A man of stature, somewhat tall and comely, with a very reverend countenance, such as the beholder must love and fear.

His hair the color of the chestnut full ripe, plain to the ears, whence downward it is more orient, curling and waving about His shoulders. In the midst of His forehead is a seam or partition after the manner of the Nazarites, forehead plain and very delicate; His face without spot or wrinkle, beautiful with a lovely red. His mouth and nose so formed as nothing can be represented. His beard thick, in color like His hair, not overlong. His look innocent and mature. His eyes gray, quick and clear.

In reproving, He is terrible, in admonishing courteous and fair spoken; pleasant in conversation, mixed with gravity.

In proportion of body, most excellent, His hands and arms delectable to behold. In speaking very temperate, modest and wise, a man of singular beauty, surpassing the children of men.

> Face to face with Christ my Savior,
> Face to face—what will it be—
> When with rapture I behold Him,
> Jesus Christ who died for me.
>
> Face to face I shall behold Him,
> Far beyond the starry sky;
> Face to face in all His glory,
> I shall see Him by and by!

(Carrie E. Breck, "Face to Face")

SOUL FOOD

Blessed are those who hunger and thirst for righteousness, for they will be filled.

—Matthew 5:6 NIV

Soul food is food which is traditionally eaten by African-Americans. Such things as chitterlings, ham hocks, and collard greens. It is called soul food because it satisfies not only the body but also the soul. For soul food arouses emotions and sentiments that give African-Americans a sense of identity.

Jesus talks about soul food in the fourth Beatitude: "Blessed are they which do hunger and thirst after righteousness: for they shall be filled." The only way to be filled with righteousness is to be filled with God. The word "fullness" is used more often in the Bible in that way than any other. Paul speaks to the Colossians of Christ, "For in Him dwelleth all the fullness of the Godhead bodily" (2:9). In the Epistle to the Ephesians he speaks of the church as the "fullness of Him that fills all in all" (1:23). In that same letter he offers this prayer for Christians: "That ye may be able to know the love of Christ, which passes knowledge, that you might be filled with all the fulness of God" (3:19).

How is one filled with God? Look again at the Beatitudes. The first says realize your spiritual poverty. The second says mourn for your sin. The third says surrender completely to God. The fourth says hunger and thirst for Him, and you will be filled.

In a biography of Abraham Lincoln, the author tells the story of the profound spiritual experience that marked the last days of the great president's life. As a blind man longs for light, Lincoln groped after a fuller, sweeter, more satisfying faith. Anyone familiar with Lincoln's speeches realizes that he was very familiar with the Bible. During those last months of his life, when his soul lay torn and bleeding like the nation itself, he said to a friend, "I have been reading the Beatitudes and can at least claim one of the blessings therein unfolded. It is the blessing pronounced upon those who hunger and thirst after righteousness." You, too, can claim that blessing.

THE MOURNER'S BENCH

Blessed are they that mourn: for they shall be comforted.

—Matthew 5:4

Through the centuries, expositors have been divided over the meaning of these words of our Lord. Some of the ancient church fathers—Clement, Chrysostom, and Jerome—held that the words refer only to mourning for sin. On the other hand, Augustine, Luther, and Calvin taught that the words refer to sorrow caused by suffering and distress.

Modern preachers take the position that the mourning in this Beatitude includes sorrow for both sin and suffering. For example, in *The Secret of Happiness*, Billy Graham's book on the Beatitudes, the evangelist talks about the mourning of inadequacy, the mourning of repentance, the mourning of love, the mourning of soul travail, and the mourning of bereavement.

Personally, I believe that this broad interpretation of the text that includes mourning for both sin and suffering is the correct one. After all, the Bible says that God is the God of all comfort. The old spiritual declares, "There is a balm in Gilead to make the wounded whole; There is a balm in Gilead to heal the sin-sick soul."

In an earlier time, churches had a special pew called the "mourner's bench" where people who had a deep concern about their soul might sit. Dr. Charles Allen, pastor of the First United Methodist Church in Houston, in his wonderful book *God's Psychiatry*, suggests that modern man has exchanged the mourner's bench for the psychiatrist's couch. Dr. Karl Menninger, a world-renowned psychiatrist, suggested a similar thing in his book *Whatever Became of Sin?*

What I am advocating is a return to the mourner's bench—not a special pew in the church, but a special place in our hearts. For anyone

223

who wants the joy of the Lord in his heart should have a mourner's bench there. As Charles Wesley said in a beloved hymn,

> I want a principle within, of watchful, godly fear;
> A sensibility of sin, a pain to feel it near.

THE HEM OF HIS GARMENT

And, behold, a woman, which was diseased with an issue of blood twelve years, came behind Him, and touched the hem of His garment; For she said within herself, If I may but touch His garment, I shall be whole.
— Matthew 9:20-21

One day in the year 1669 Sir Isaac Newton completed work on the first reflecting telescope. He stood before his invention and peered through the eyepiece to behold things which no human eye had ever before seen. In the excitement of that historic moment, he turned to an assistant standing beside him and said, "I have just caught hold of the skirts of God." For Sir Isaac Newton the wonder and beauty of the heavens was the hem of His garment.

And there is a similar need for each of us to catch hold of the skirts of God. For we cannot see God or the blessed Savior who has redeemed us. We must say as it was said of Samuel in his day that there is no more open vision. We cannot speak with God face to face as Moses did. We cannot say as the apostle John said, "That which was from the beginning, which we have heard, which we have seen with our eyes, which we have looked upon, and our hands have handled, of the Word of life" (1 John 1:1). No, we cannot see God. But the fact remains that our greatest need is for intimate, personal fellowship with Him.

No, we cannot see God, but we can touch the hem of His garment. And the effect is the same. For Jesus said to this poor woman who only touched the hem of His garment, "Thy faith hath made thee whole" (Matt. 9:22). And my friend, this is all that Christ can do for any of us. He did as much for this woman as He did when he reached forth to touch the body of Jairus' daughter. He made them each whole.

And so the Word of God teaches us that although we do not have exactly the same relationship to Jesus Christ our God as did His apostles, nevertheless, our experience with Him can be as real, meaningful, and vital as theirs. We can only touch the hem of His garment, but we can be made whole. Jesus said to His apostles, "Because you have seen me, you have believed; Blessed are those who have not seen and yet have believed" (John 20:29). And so, let us reach out in hope and faith and touch the hem of His garment that we might be made whole.

FREE AT LAST

So if the Son sets you free, you will be free indeed.

—John 8:36 NIV

If you have seen the movie *The Three Faces of Eve,* you are familiar with the idea of multiple personalities. In the movie a psychiatrist discovers that his patient, Eve White, has two additional personalities who were known as Eve Black and Jane. What you may not have realized as you watched the movie is that it was based on an actual clinical history from a psychiatrist's casebook.

In cases of multiple personality the individual has two or more distinguishable personalities. In one personality the individual may, for example, be happy and carefree; in another, anxious and sullen. The personalities shift back and forth, but each retains its separate identity.

In a story from Luke 8:26-39 we have not only a case of multiple personality, but also a case of demon possession. Demons, like their master, Satan, are fallen angels. Demons are to Satan what angels are to God.

Do demons really exist? If you saw the movie *The Exorcist,* you saw a pretty convincing presentation of a case for their existence. The movie deals with the rite of exorcism or casting out demons as it is practiced in the Roman Catholic Church and tells the story of a twentieth-century priest who is called upon to exorcize a demon from a teenage girl.

Most of us will never see a demon-possessed man, I suppose, but there are a lot of things in our modern culture that come pretty close. Alcoholism is one of those. There is nothing that demonstrates the power of the gospel more dramatically than the conversion of an alcoholic, and I have known many of those. In the church that we served in Michigan there was a man who attended who was the superintendent of construction at the nearby airbase. He had been a hard-working, hard-driving, hard-drinking man all of his adult years. Then one Sunday evening he attended the service in a little Southern Baptist church in Omaha. When the invitation to receive Christ was given this big man walked down the aisle of the church and, like the man in this story, fell on his knees. He never took a drink after that and the Lord used him in several places to help churches construct new buildings. It's true. "If the Son shall make you free, you shall be free indeed."

There is an old gospel song that puts it so well:

I would love to tell you what I think of Jesus
Since I found in Him a friend so kind and true;
I would tell you how He changed my life completely—
He did something that no other friend could do.

No one ever cared for me like Jesus,
There's no other friend so kind as He;
No one else could take the sin and darkness from me—
O how much He cared for me!
(C. F. Weigle, "No One Ever Cared for Me Like Jesus")

THE MAN WHO CAME

Jesus said, "But go and learn what this means: 'I desire mercy, not sacrifice.' For I have not come to call the righteous, but sinners."
—Matthew 9:13 NIV

In a sermon titled "The Most Unique Character in History" Dr. Oswald J. Smith, late pastor of the People's Church in Toronto, points out that no man was ever born like Jesus, no man ever lived like Jesus, no man ever taught like Jesus, no man ever worked like Jesus, and no man ever died like Jesus. It is the uniqueness of His birth that I am thinking of today. Not the fact that He was born of a virgin. Not the fact that His birth was prophesied centuries beforehand. But simply the fact that of only one man's birth in history is it said, "He came." Other men were born. Jesus Christ came.

Now there are many questions that we could ask about that great truth. We could ask *How did He come?* and ponder the mystery of His virgin birth. We could ask *Who was it who came?* and delve into the wonder and the glory of the incarnation. But it seems to me that the most important question of all is *Why did He come?* Why did He come "out of the ivory palaces and into a world of woe"?

Various answers have been given to that question. Some would say that He came to be a great teacher. And He was that. Are there any words in the literature of the world that compare in beauty and truth with the Sermon on the Mount? Others would say that He came to be our moral example. And He was that. Of what other person can it be said, "He knew no sin?" Still others would say that He came to be a social reformer. And He was that. I daresay that more heavy burdens have been lifted from more weary backs in the name of Jesus than any other.

Why did He come? I think that it is important to know what Jesus Himself had to say about that subject. One day I took my well-worn

Young's Analytical Concordance to the Bible and looked up every reference in the Gospels where Jesus speaks of His coming to earth. To the best of my knowledge there are nineteen such verses. The first is Matthew 5:17, " I am not come to destroy, but to fulfill." The last is John 18:37, "For this cause came I into the world."

As I analyzed these verses I discovered an amazing fact. Of the nineteen verses in the Gospels where Jesus speaks of His coming to earth, thirteen of them make reference to sin. So, if we would have Christ's own answer to the question as to why He came we must say that He came to earth to deal with the sin of humanity. And He also died for you and me. In the Epistle to the Romans Paul declares, "God demonstrates His own love for us in this: While we were still sinners, Christ died for us" (Rom. 5:8 NIV).

RAGS TO RICHES

Blessed are the poor in spirit: for theirs is the kingdom of heaven.
—Matthew 5:3

To be blessed means to be favored by God. That concept is very important in understanding the Beatitudes. The New International Version has retained the word "blessed" in the Beatitudes, whereas many modern translations use the word "happy." But the word "happy" comes from the word "happen" which suggests that one's feelings of joy depend upon the circumstances of one's life. That is not what the word "blessed" means. The ancient Greek historian Herodotus used the word to describe an oasis. The Christian life is like an oasis in the desert. Regardless of our surroundings, we rejoice because of the life of God within.

Who are the poor in spirit? Tertullian, one of the ancient church fathers, translates the first Beatitude, "Blessed are the beggars, for theirs is the Kingdom of Heaven."

In New York Harbor stands the Statue of Liberty, the symbol of American freedom. Inscribed on the statue are these words: "Give me your tired, your poor, your huddled masses yearning to breathe free, the wretched refuse of your teeming shore, send these, the homeless, tempest tossed to me." Such is the Kingdom of God. Jesus said, "I am not come to call the righteous, but sinners to repentance" (Matt. 9:13b) and "Him that cometh to me I will in no wise cast out" (John 6:37b). "Blessed are the poor in spirit, for theirs is the Kingdom of Heaven."

If you would enter that Kingdom, you need only offer the Billy Graham Prayer. Millions of people have done that and found Christ and His Kingdom.

Dear Lord Jesus, I know that I am a sinner and need Your forgiveness. I believe that You died for my sins. I want to turn from my sins. I now invite You to come into my heart and life. I want to trust and follow You as Lord and Savior. In Jesus' name. Amen.

Jesus, I my cross have taken,
All to leave and follow thee.
Destitute, despised, forsaken,
Thou from hence, my all shall be.
Perish every fond ambition,
All I've sought and hoped and known,
Yet, how rich is my condition,
God and heaven are still my own.

(Henry F. Lyte, "Jesus, I My Cross Have Taken")

THE CROSSROADS OF LIFE

Enter through the narrow gate. For wide is the gate and broad is the road that leads to destruction, and many enter through it.

—Matthew 7:13 NIV

Yogi Berra said it: "If you come to a fork in the road, take it." That may sound like typical Yogi Berra double talk, but there is an element of truth in it. That is to say that there are those times in life's journey in which we are forced to make choices.

Robert Frost points that out in his beloved poem "The Road Less Traveled":

Two roads diverged in a wood, and I—
I took the one less traveled by,
And that has made all the difference.

And what is the difference? As someone has put it, "The reason that the broad way is not the best way is because it's so crowded."

Charlie Brown spoke for many when he responded to Psychiatrist Lucy's remark. Charlie said, "But I don't want any downs. I only want ups."

On the other hand, it is the narrow way that teaches discipline and imparts character. As Phillips translates, "When all kinds of trials and temptations crowd into your lives...don't resent them as intruders, but welcome them as friends! Realize that they come to test and to produce in you the quality of endurance" (James 1:2-3 Phillips).

Man may trouble and distress me, 'twill but drive me to Thy Breast:
Life with trials hard may press me, heaven will bring me sweeter rest.

O 'tis not in grief to harm me, while Thy love is left to me;
O'twere not in joy to charm me, were that joy unmixed with Thee.

(Henry F. Lyte, "Jesus, I My Cross Have Taken")

DOES YOUR CONSCIENCE BOTHER YOU?

My conscience is clear, but that does not make me innocent. It is the Lord who judges me.

—1 Corinthians 4:4 NIV

When I was a pastor in Michigan I took a course from Central Michigan University entitled "The Psychology of Behavior Problems in Children." There were about fifteen people in the class, all of them public school teachers except the Roman Catholic chaplain from nearby Wurtsmith Air Force Base and myself. One evening the professor began the class by asking everyone in the room to give a definition of the word "conscience." He wrote our definitions on the blackboard as we gave them. Most of the definitions had somewhat negative connotations.

When everyone had given their definition and the professor had written them all on the blackboard, he said, "If conscience is all of these bad things that you say it is, then why don't we just do away with conscience?" Then, very dramatically, he drew a big X over everything that he had written on the blackboard.

Now, whether he believed that or was just trying to provoke discussion I am not sure. But, as a matter of fact, there are a great many people today who would like to do away with conscience, their own and everybody else's. We are living in an age characterized by permissiveness and relativism in morals.

The dictionary defines conscience as the internal recognition of right and wrong as regards one's actions and motives. The Bible teaches that conscience is a God-given faculty. In Romans 2:15 Paul says of the heathen who do not have the law, "They show that what the law requires is written on their hearts, while their conscience also bears witness." George Washington put it well when he said, "Labor to keep alive in your heart that little spark of celestial fire—conscience."

The question is, "How can I know if my conscience is leading me in the right direction?" Someone has said that following your conscience is like following your nose, it depends on which way it is pointed. We need some guide outside of ourselves to point our conscience in the right direction.

We had in our church in Michigan a young officer who was a navigator on a B-52 bomber. He explained to me once how he did his work. Every hour or so he would leave his charts and maps behind in his windowless cubbyhole beneath the cockpit and go up to the cockpit with his sextant and take a reading on the stars. You see, he needed something outside of the plane to tell him that he was on the right course.

Our situation in life is like that. "We walk by faith and not by sight" (2 Cor. 5:7). We need something outside of ourselves to guide us through life. Our conscience must be pointed in the right direction. For the Christian the Bible, the Word of God, is that guide.

GOD'S UNKNOWN SOLDIERS

Who through faith conquered kingdoms, administered justice, and gained what was promised; who shut the mouths of lions, quenched the fury of the flames, and escaped the edge of the sword; whose weakness was turned to strength; and who became powerful in battle and routed foreign armies.

—Hebrews 11:33-34 NIV

One day, for whatever reason, I attempted to recall the military cemeteries we had visited in our travels. Fortunately, my faithful editor, Sylvia, had already compiled such a list. The list included such places as Gettysburg from the Civil War, Verdun in France where a million men were killed in World War I, and Omaha Beach from World War II.

These all bring to mind Captain John D. McCrae's poem "In Flanders Field":

In Flanders fields the poppies blow
Between the crosses, row on row,
That mark our place; and in the sky
The larks, still bravely singing, fly
Scarce heard amid the guns below.

Take up our quarrel with the foe!
To you from failing hands, we throw
The torch—Be yours to hold it high!
If ye break faith with us who die
We shall not sleep, though poppies grow
In Flanders field.

Of all the memorial cemeteries that we visited, the most meaningful to me is Arlington. Six men from my company are buried there in a common grave. The body of John F. Kennedy is buried there. And the Tomb of the Unknown Soldier is there with its inscription: "Here lies the body of a soldier known only to God."

Does God have His unknown soldiers? Apparently so. Hebrews 11 is the Faith Chapter of the Bible, sometimes called God's Hall of Fame. The author demonstrates the meaning of faith in the lives of some of the best known characters from the Old Testament. He concludes the chapter, however, by referring to the exploits of nameless prophets—God's Unknown Soldiers.

Yesterday I received a blood transfusion, my seventy-sixth unit in the last three years. The truth of the matter is that I owe my life to these seventy-six people, even though I do not know their names. I give thanks to God for these unknown soldiers. Some of the most important work that God has done is not remembered. Who knows the name of the person who led William Carey, the Father of Modern Missions, to Christ? Who remembers the uneducated farmer who was responsible for the conversion of Spurgeon? Who remembers the preacher who brought the sermon when Billy Graham made his decision for Christ?

> Faith of our fathers! Living still in spite of dungeon, fire and sword.
> O how our hearts beat high with joy when e'er we hear that glorious word!
> Faith of our fathers, holy faith! We will be true to thee till death!
>
> Faith of our fathers! We will love both friend and foe in all our strife.
> And preach thee, too, as love knows how, by kindly words and virtuous life.
> Faith of our fathers, holy faith! We will be true to thee till death!
> (Frederick W. Faber, "Faith of Our Fathers")

GOD'S RIGHT HAND

But I think it is necessary to send back to you Epaphroditus, my brother, fellow worker and fellow soldier, who is also your messenger, whom you sent to take care of my needs.

—Philippians 2:25 NIV

On one occasion the chairman of the department of philosophy in a Midwestern university said to me regarding his former secretary, "That girl was my right hand for seven years." By that he meant, of course, that this young lady's service was so indispensable as to make her as valuable as his own right hand. Most people in positions of responsibility would freely acknowledge the existence of such people in their work.

God must also have his right-hand men and women. There are many people in the Bible deserving of that accolade: Abraham, the friend of God; David, the man after God's own heart; Moses, the servant of the Lord; John, the disciple whom Jesus loved; and certainly Paul himself.

I would like to suggest, however, that there are also numerous little people in the Bible who deserve such recognition. People that Peter Marshall called "Saints of the Rank and File." Among these I would suggest Epaphroditus. Now at first glance it may not appear that Epaphroditus is especially noteworthy. He is mentioned only twice in the New Testament: in Philippians 4:18 and 4:25. Even then it is only in the capacity of Paul's helper.

However, as Spurgeon said, "It takes more grace that I can tell to play the second fiddle well." As a matter of fact, there are no second fiddles in God's orchestra. Whoever does God's work in God's way for God's glory is God's right hand. For a Christian is a mind through which Christ thinks, a voice through which Christ speaks, a heart through which Christ loves, and a hand through which Christ helps.

There is a beautiful story about Henry Drummond, the author of the most famous gospel tract ever written, "The Greatest Thing in the World." It is an exposition of 1 Corinthians 13, the Love Chapter of the Bible. It seems that a young man applied for membership in a church in England. He was being interviewed by the deacons of the church regarding his Christian experience. He explained that he had been converted through the influence of Henry Drummond. At the mention of this famous name the deacons became very interested and one of them asked, "What did Mr. Drummond say that caused you to be converted?" The young man replied, "Well, he didn't say anything. He just put his hand on my shoulder."

When a man ain't got a friend and is feelin' kinda blue,
And the clouds hang low and heavy and won't let the sunshine through,
'Tis a great thing, O my brother, for a fellow just to lay
His hand upon your shoulder in a friendly sort of way.
Now this world's a curious compound with its honey and its gall,
With its care and bitter crosses, but a good world after all.
And a good God must have made it; leastwise that is what I say
When His hand is on my shoulder in a friendly sort of way.

NICE GUYS FINISH FIRST

Blessed are the meek: for they shall inherit the earth.

—Matthew 5:5

Let me give you an example from the world of sports that illustrates exactly what the Bible means by the meek. Vince Lombardi was for many years coach of the Green Bay Packers, and many would say he was the greatest coach ever in professional football. What you may not know is that before he was a football coach, Lombardi coached basketball at Fordham University. He had a particular technique that he used with basketball players to remind them that he was in charge. Each day before practice he would line the players up at the edge of the court and say to them, "Every man who wants to play basketball take one step forward." Then, of course, everybody stepped into the playing court. Then Lombardi would say, "Now you belong to me." By that he meant, "If you play on my team, you do exactly as I say." That is what it means to be meek in biblical terms—to be completely surrendered to Jesus Christ, to belong to Him, to do exactly as He says.

Listen to the testimony of two people who possessed more of this earth than almost any others who ever lived—Napoleon and Queen Victoria. Napoleon said, "Caesar, Alexander, Charlemagne and I tried to conquer the world by force and we failed. Jesus Christ conquers by love and at this hour there are millions who would gladly die for Him." Victoria said, "If Jesus Christ should return to earth today, I would lay the crowns of the British Empire at His feet."

The Scripture says, "The earth is the Lord's and the fulness thereof; the world and they that dwell therein" (Psalm 24:1). The earth is His and we are His. Therefore, the earth is ours—if we belong to Him. For we are the heirs of God and joint heirs with Christ. That applies not only to the material world, but above all to the spiritual world. Life consists not in what a man possesses, but in what possesses him. Who really inherited the earth? Alexander the Great, who at the age of thirty sat down and wept because he had no more worlds to conquer? Or the apostle Paul, who wrote from his Roman prison cell, "I have learned in whatsoever state I am therewith to be content" (Phil. 4:11b) and "I can do all things through Christ who strengthens me" (4:13)?

EYEWITNESS OF HIS MAJESTY

Above all, you must understand that no prophecy of Scripture came about by the prophet's own interpretation. For prophecy never had its origin in the will of man, but men spoke from God as they were carried along by the Holy Spirit.

—2 Peter 1:20-21 NIV

In this passage of Scripture, the apostle Peter refers to one of the notable experiences of his life—his witness of the transfiguration of our Lord. For you will remember that on one occasion our Savior took with him Peter and James and John and went into a high mountain to pray. While He was praying, He was transfigured before them. There appeared unto Him Elijah and Moses and a voice from heaven declared, "This is my beloved son, in whom I am well pleased." Thus, Peter could say in 2 Peter 1:16, "For we have not followed cunningly devised fables, when we made known unto you the power and coming of our Lord Jesus, but were eyewitnesses of His majesty."

We would all like to have been eyewitnesses of His majesty. However, as wonderful and great as such an experience might have been it is not the ultimate proof of the truth and reality of the gospel of Jesus Christ, nor is it the highest form of Christian experience. For, having said that he was an eyewitness to these things, Peter goes on to add in verse 19, "We have also a more sure word of prophecy."

What could be more important than being an eyewitness to the events of the gospel? Peter answers that question by pointing to the living Word of God. "For the prophecy came not in old time by the will of men: but holy men of God spake as they were moved by the Holy Ghost" (1:21). In other words, any man who takes up the sacred Scriptures to read them and to meditate upon them and to pray over them and to obey them is just as much an eyewitness to the majesty of Jesus Christ as those who lived when Jesus was here among men. For you see, if ever there was a time when the voice of God is heard, it is when His Word is read.

Because its divine character is evident in its ability to change human lives, we should "Be doers of the Word and not hearers only" (James 1:22). For, you see, the best proof of the inspiration of the Bible is the inspiring lives of those who read it.

You are writing a gospel, a chapter each day,
By deeds that you do, by words that you say.
Men read what you write, whether faithless or true.
Say, what is the gospel according to you?
(from "The Gospel According To You," author unknown)

MY FATHER'S HOUSE

Surely, goodness and mercy shall follow me all the days of my life; and I will dwell in the house of the Lord forever.

—Psalm 23:6

Psalm 23 is known as the Shepherd Psalm. However, beginning at verse 5 David changes the metaphor from that of the shepherd and his sheep to that of a host and his guest. In the Middle East it was the custom to anoint the head of a guest with oil as a symbol of honor and respect. So David writes of God, "You anoint my head with oil" (v. 5). Food and drink were in abundance on such an occasion. So David writes, "My cup runs over" (v. 5). As long as a guest remained under the roof of his host he was provided protection from his enemies. So David writes, "You prepare a table before me in the presence of my enemies" (v. 5).

Jesus also used the image that David employed here, that is, of the believer as a guest in God's house. In the fourteenth chapter of John's Gospel the writer describes Jesus' final conversation with the disciples before He went to the cross. He tells them that He is going to leave them. They are very anxious and upset. He speaks to them these beautiful words, "Let not your hearts be troubled. You believe in God. Believe also in me. In my Father's house are many rooms. If it were not so I would have told you. I go to prepare a place for you and if I go and prepare a place for you, I will come again and receive you unto myself that where I am there you may be also" (John 14:1-3).

Jesus taught us that we are not simply guests in God's house but that we are His children. The Bible says, "To all who received Him [Christ], who believed in His name, He gave power to become children of God" (John 1:12 RSV). Heaven, then, is the Christian's home.

It was Billy Graham who told the story of a little girl who was seen going into a cemetery just as dark was falling. Some adults picnicking nearby asked her, "Aren't you afraid to go into the cemetery after dark?" The little girl replied, "Oh no, I'm not afraid because, you see, my home is just on the other side." So it is for the Christian; death is simply going home.

> All the way my Savior leads me;
> What have I to ask beside?
> Can I doubt His tender mercy
> Who through life has been my Guide?
>
> All the way my Savior leads me
> Oh, the fullness of his love!
> Perfect rest to me is promised
> In my Father's house above.
>
> (Fanny J. Crosby, "All the Way My Savior Leads Me")

THE BIBLE READER'S DIGEST

For God so loved the world, that he gave his only begotten Son, that whosoever believes in Him should not perish, but have everlasting life.
—John 3:16

The Reader's Digest is the most popular magazine in America today. And it very well deserves to be, for it saves us both time and money. This appeals to the average American, for *The Reader's Digest* selects the best of current periodical literature and puts it between two covers. And all of this for a reasonable price.

Those of you who have studied this ponderous volume that we call the Holy Bible, which is really a divine library of sixty-six books, have doubtless wished at some time or other for a *Bible Reader's Digest*—some book that would condense the more important teachings of the Bible into less space. It should be of interest to you, then, to learn that we have just such a *Bible Reader's Digest*. It was given to us by God Himself and is to be found within the pages of the Holy Bible itself. It is not a book of the Bible. It is not a chapter of the Bible. It is not even a paragraph of the Bible. It is one verse of the Bible. This one verse has been called the Bible in one verse, the Gospel in a nutshell, or as I have chosen to call it, the *Bible Reader's Digest*. That verse is John 3:16—"For God so loved the world that He gave His only begotten Son that whosoever believes in Him, should not perish but have everlasting life." Yes, this is the Bible in one verse and the *Bible Reader's Digest*. Therefore, we should give special heed to this verse. For John 3:16 contains the three most important truths in the Bible.

This verse contains the greatest facts of the Bible. First, it says that God loves sinners. "For God so loved the world." Christ died for sinners. "That He gave His only begotten Son." And that faith saves sinners. "That whosoever believes in Him should not perish but have everlasting life." Yes, John 3:16 is the message of the Bible.

247

But more important than that, John 3:16 is God's message for you. A gentleman by the name of John Smith said, "I am glad that when God wrote John 3:16, He did not say that if John Smith should believe in him he should not perish, because if he would have said that I would not have known which of the many John Smith's He meant. But the fact that He said whosoever causes me to realize that God meant me." And so it is that when God said whosoever, He meant you. God loves you. Christ died for you. Faith will save you.

Wonderful things in the Bible I see,
This is the dearest that Jesus loves me.
                    (Philip P. Bliss, "Jesus Loves Even Me")

Wonderful things in the Bible are true,
But this is the dearest that Jesus loves you.

STRANGERS AND PILGRIMS

Dear friends, I urge you, as aliens and strangers in the world, to abstain from sinful desires, which war against your soul.

1 Peter 2:11 NIV

Though we are strangers in this world, we are to live as heavenly pilgrims. Here in this passage of Scripture, Peter offers several guideposts to proper Christian conduct. The first question that Peter would have us ask about our conduct is this: *Does it glorify God?* In verse 12 we read, "Live such good lives among the pagans that, though they accuse you of doing wrong, they may see your good deeds and glorify God on the day He visits us" (1 Peter 2:12 NIV).

And then a second guidepost to moral conduct for Christian pilgrims is this: *Is it the will of God?* In verse 15 Peter writes, "For so is the will of God that with well doing ye may put to silence the ignorance of foolish men."

A third question that a heavenly pilgrim might consider as a guideline to conduct in this pagan world is: *Is it worthy of a servant of God?* In verse 16 Peter writes, "As free, and not using your liberty as a cloak of maliciousness, but as the servants of God."

There is a fourth guidepost for heavenly pilgrims on their journey through this pagan world, and that is the question: *Is it right with your conscience?* In verse 19 of this second chapter Peter writes, "For this is thankworthy if a man for conscience toward God endure grief, suffering wrongfully."

And then there is a final question I would ask, a guidepost for heavenly pilgrims to order their conduct in a sinful world: *Does it follow the example of Christ?* In verse 21 Peter writes, "For even hereunto were ye called: because Christ also suffered for us, leaving us an example, that ye should follow His steps." Certainly the final test of Christian conduct ought to be, Is this the thing that Jesus Christ would do?

Hudson Taylor, founder of the China Inland Mission, gave us this advice: "Be God's man or woman in God's place, doing God's work at God's time in God's way."

GREATER LOVE

Greater love has no man than this, that a man lay down his life for his friends.

—John 15:13

On High Street in Soham, England, where our son Steve lives, there is an obelisk some twenty feet high. On its four sides are inscribed the names of the men of that village who were killed or died in the Great War of 1914-18. Our daughter-in-law's grandfather's name is there. Across the bottom of the monument are these words from John 15:13, "Greater love has no man than this that a man lay down his life for his friends." In every village in England, no matter how small, you will find a similar monument honoring the dead of that war. Each year on November 11, known as Remembrance Day in England, the people of the village gather at that monument to honor those men who gave their lives for their country.

Not fifty yards from the monument in Soham, another memorial is maintained, for there is the Soham Baptist Church. The memorial there relates to a passage from the Epistle to the Romans. Paul says, "But God demonstrates His own love toward us, in that while we were still sinners, Christ died for us" (Rom. 5:8 NKJV). The memorial at the Baptist church is called by some Holy Communion and by others the Lord's Supper.

Several years ago Sylvia and I attended an International Ecumenical Seminar at the International Baptist Theological Seminary in Prague, and we decided to stay on in the Czech Republic to visit some places that we had not had time to visit during the conference. That Sunday we attended the service at the seminary. A new group of people had assembled for the next conference. There were about one hundred people in attendance. The worship leader asked people during the service to come to a map of the world on the wall of the chapel and point to the country from which they had come. We counted twenty-one different countries represented in that congregation. That is the central message of our Christian faith. "For God so loved the world that He gave His only begotten Son that whosoever believes in Him should not perish but have everlasting life" (John 3:16).

MAN'S MOST DIVINE ACT

From that time on Jesus began to preach, "Repent, for the kingdom of heaven is near."

—Matthew 4:17 NIV

A great many people have difficulty accepting the fact that David is described in the Bible as a man after God's own heart. "How," they ask, "can a man who has committed murder and adultery be a man after God's own heart?"

I think that Psalm 51 answers that question for us. This psalm is David's prayer of confession following his repentance of those sins. Repentance is close to the heart of God. For does not Scripture say, "There is joy in the presence of the angels of God over one sinner that repents" (Luke 15:10)? As Thomas Carlyle said, "Of all the acts of man, repentance is the most divine."

The importance of repentance is emphasized throughout the Bible. Jonah preached repentance in Nineveh until the whole city turned to God. The prophet Ezekiel preached repentance to Israel, "Repent, and turn yourselves from all your transgressions, so iniquity shall not be your ruin," he said (Ezek. 18:30b). The great message of John the Baptist, the forerunner of Christ, was repentance. He said, "Repent for the Kingdom of God is at hand" (Matt. 3:2). Jesus said, "Except you repent you shall all likewise perish" (Luke 13:3). The sermon that Peter preached on the day of Pentecost was, "Repent, and be baptized everyone of you in the name of Jesus Christ for the remission of sins" (Acts 2:38). Paul described his ministry by saying that he "testified both to the Jews and also to the Greeks, repentance toward God, and faith toward our Lord Jesus Christ" (Acts 20:21). All in all, repentance is mentioned seventy times in the New Testament.

What is repentance? The classic definition of repentance is that of Augustus Hopkins Strong: "Repentance is that voluntary change in the mind of the sinner in which he turns from sin. Being essentially a change of mind, it involves a change of view, a change of feeling and a change of purpose." Spurgeon provided this description of repentance: "It is a change of mind of the most thorough and radical sort, and it is attended with sorrow for the past, and resolve of amendment for the future."

> Repentance is to leave
> The sins we loved before;
> And show that we in earnest grieve
> By doing so no more.

The best illustration of the meaning of repentance that I know comes from the ministry of Dr. Walter A. Maier, the first Lutheran Hour preacher and professor of Old Testament at Concordia Lutheran Seminary. One Sunday he was preaching on repentance. A young wife and mother was driving along the highway on her way to a secret rendezvous with her illicit lover. She turned on her radio and the voice of Walter Maier came on saying, "Stop, right where you are. Turn around and go back." The young woman came under conviction of sin and did just what Dr. Maier said. She made a U-turn and returned home to her husband and children. Later she wrote to tell Dr. Maier of her repentance. That's repentance. Stop. Right where you are. Turn around and go back.

THE MESSIAH

For to us a child is born, to us a son is given, and the government will be on His shoulders. And he will be called Wonderful Counselor, Mighty God, Everlasting Father, Prince of Peace.

—Isaiah 9:6 NIV

In this passage of Scripture we have the royal title of the promised Messiah—King of Israel. These words are familiar to many because of a magnificent chorus in Handel's *Messiah*. Throughout the centuries Christians have believed that Jesus Christ, our Lord and Savior, King of Kings and Lord of Lords, is the ultimate fulfillment of these beautiful words.

I think first of *His wonderful teachings*. His name shall be called "Wonderful Counselor." In modern times many have found the teachings of Jesus a source of challenge and inspiration. When Mahatma Gandhi was a law student at the University of London, he bought a Bible and began to read it. He got as far as the book of Numbers in the Old Testament and decided to try the New Testament. He found the New Testament more interesting and said, "The Sermon on the Mount went straight to my heart." It was on the basis of the teachings in the Sermon on the Mount that Gandhi transformed the lives of hundreds of millions of people in India and throughout the world.

Then, I believe that Jesus of Nazareth is the Messiah of whom Isaiah wrote because of *His mighty miracles*. His name shall be called "Mighty God."

Then, I believe that Jesus of Nazareth is the Messiah of whom Isaiah spoke because of *His everlasting love*. His name shall be called "Everlasting Father." No one taught us more about the Fatherhood of God than Jesus. No one taught us more about the love of God than He did.

Finally, I believe that Jesus of Nazareth is the Messiah-King of whom Isaiah wrote because of *His perfect peace.* His name shall be called "Prince of Peace." I say perfect peace because that is the expression that Isaiah used in 26:3—"Thou wilt keep him in perfect peace whose mind is stayed on Thee."

Although that peace among nations has not come, there is a peace which Christ gives even in the midst of the world's tribulation. He said, "My peace I give unto you, not as the world gives" (John 14:27b). It was this peace that Paul described from his Roman prison cell as "the peace of God which passes all understanding shall keep your hearts and minds through Christ Jesus" (Phil. 4:7).

His name shall be called "Prince of Peace."

I believe that if you earnestly seek the answer to the question "What do you think of Jesus Christ?" that you will soon agree with John, the disciple whom Jesus loved, "That which was from the beginning, which we have heard, which we have seen with our eyes, which we have looked upon and our hands have handled, of the Word of Life" (1 John 1:1), and with Peter, the rock upon which the church is built, "You are the Christ, the Son of the Living God" (Matt. 16:16 NIV).

THE BEGINNING
OF THE GOSPEL

The time is fulfilled, and the kingdom of God is at hand. Repent, and believe in the gospel.

—Mark 1:15 NKJV

"The beginning of the gospel of Jesus Christ, the Son of God" (Mark 1:1). Thus begins the first written record of the life and ministry of our Lord Jesus Christ. The generally accepted view today is that Mark wrote his gospel before Matthew, Luke, and John, probably from Rome sometime between the years 65 and 70 A.D.

In the prologue to the Gospel we are told of the divine preparation for the public ministry of Jesus. Mark points to the Old Testament Scriptures, the testimony of John the Baptist, and Jesus' temptation in the wilderness as a necessary prelude to the work of Christ described in his Gospel. When these things had come to pass Jesus came preaching, saying, "The time is fulfilled, the Kingdom of God is at hand; repent and believe the gospel" (Mark 1:15). And so it is that, just as God determined the events and circumstances of Jesus' life and ministry, so He prepares the hearts of men and women today to receive Christ and the gospel. "The time is fulfilled, the Kingdom of God is at hand; repent and believe the gospel."

This is the message of holy Scripture and it has power to reach the hearts of men and women. On one occasion when we were in London, Sylvia and I attended a performance of the one-man show *St. Mark's Gospel* by the well-known British actor Alex McCowan. Dressed in a business suit, with no props except a table, two chairs, and a King James New Testament ("just in case"), he simply recited the Gospel of Mark in a three hour performance. It was a very moving experience for everyone. Think of it. For three years in a regular London theater, six nights a week, this man had been simply reciting the Gospel of Mark at well-attended performances. You see, this beautiful story touches the hearts of men and women and changes their lives.

> I love to tell the story
> Because it did so much for me;
> And that is just the reason
> I tell it now to thee.
>
> (A. Catherine Hankey, "I Love to Tell the Story")

MIGHTY GRACE

Blessed is he whose transgressions are forgiven, whose sins are covered.
Blessed is the man whose sin the LORD does not count against him and in
whose spirit is no deceit.

—Psalm 32:1-2 NIV

On one occasion Charles Spurgeon, the famous pastor of the Metropolitan Tabernacle in London during the closing years of the nineteenth century, had a dream in which he died and went to heaven. He found himself standing outside the pearly gates on that great day when the saints came marching in. He noticed that people entered the celestial city by designated groups. The first to enter were the apostles: Peter, James, John, and the rest. Spurgeon said, "I do not belong with those noble men." Next came the band of martyrs, those men and women who had laid down their lives for the cause of Christ. Spurgeon said, "I cannot join with them." Group after group went by, but none with whom Spurgeon could identify. Finally, a great host of people appeared at the gates led by our Lord Jesus Himself. On His right was the repentant thief and on His left the woman taken in adultery. A mighty shout of triumph went up for them. Spurgeon turned to an angel standing nearby and inquired, "Pray tell me, who are these?"

"These," said the angel, "are the mighty sinners saved by mighty grace."

"Here, too, I may enter," said Spurgeon. And then he awoke.

Psalm 32 was a favorite of St. Augustine. As a matter of fact, as he lay dying, he asked that the words of the first two verses of the Psalm be written on the wall of his room so that as he passed from this life to the next he might carry with him the promise of God's forgiveness.

Augustine had been saved from a life of debauchery. He lived in an illicit relationship with his teenage cousin. One day, quite by chance, or so we might say, he opened a copy of the Epistle to the Romans and read this verse: "Put on the Lord Jesus Christ and make not provision for the flesh to fulfill the lusts thereof" (13:14). In that moment his life was changed and he became, in time, one of the great saints of Christendom.

There is a tradition that some days after his conversion Augustine was walking through the streets of his native city when his former mistress saw him from a distance. She called to him but he continued on as though he did not hear her. She continued to call until she overtook him and plucked at the sleeve of his tunic. "Augustine, it is I," she said. Without looking at her, Augustine replied, "But it is not I" and walked on. As Paul said to the Corinthian Christians, "If any man be in Christ, he is a new creation; old things are passed away; behold, all things are become new" (2 Cor. 5:17).

> He breaks the power of cancelled sin;
> He sets the prisoner free.
> His blood can make the foulest clean;
> His blood availed for me.
>   (Charles Wesley, "O for a Thousand Tongues")

These are the mighty sinners saved by mighty grace. Here, too, I may enter. And so may you.

WHAT WILL YOU DO WITH JESUS?

When Jesus came out wearing the crown of thorns and the purple robe,
Pilate said to them, "Here is the man!"

—John 19:5

I suppose that there have been as many sermons preached on the question "What think ye of Christ?" as on any text in the Bible. And it is an important question.

As important as that question is, however, there is one that is even more important. That is the question that Pilate asked the mob after his private interview with our Lord: "What will you do with Jesus?" That is the more important question, you see, because it is entirely possible for a man to think rightly about Jesus but not act accordingly.

That was the case with the three principal figures in the eighteenth chapter of John: Judas Iscariot, Simon Peter, and Pontius Pilate. They each thought well of Jesus but their actions were not always in harmony with their thinking. After his betrayal of Jesus, Judas took the blood money and threw it on the floor of the temple in the presence of the priests and said, "I have sinned in that I have betrayed innocent blood" (Matt. 27:4). His thinking was right but his actions were wrong. Simon Peter was the first of the apostles to confess Jesus as the Messiah. He said to the Lord, "Thou art the Christ, the Son of the living God" (Matt. 16:16). Yet, Peter denied the Lord not once, but three times. His thinking was right but his actions were wrong. And even Pontius Pilate held Jesus in high regard. In front of the screaming mob he declared, "I find in Him no fault at all" (John 19:38). And yet he sentenced Jesus to be crucified. His thinking was right but his actions were wrong. Thus, the importance of the question, "What will you do with Jesus?"

On one occasion two men were driving down a country road and stopped to ask a farmer for directions. He said, "Go to the end of this road and turn right." So the two men drove to the end of the road, but the driver turned left. The man who was not driving said, "Why did you turn left? The man said to turn right." The driver replied, "I know he said to turn right. But he pointed left and I have learned that when a man talks one way and acts another that you should always go by the way he acts rather than by what he says."

> What will you do with Jesus?
> Neutral you cannot be;
> Someday your heart will be asking,
> "What will He do with me?"
>   (Albert B. Simpson, "What Will You Do With Jesus?")

THE QUESTION OF QUESTIONS

If a man die, shall he live again?

—Job 14:14a

When the American author Gertrude Stein lay dying in Paris, she looked up to her dearest friend standing beside her bed and asked, "What's the answer?" When her friend did not reply she asked, "Then what's the question?"

The question, of course, which every person must be concerned with in the hour of death and many times before is the question posed by Job 14:14, "If a man die, shall he live again?"

The book of Job is probably the oldest book in the Bible. This question is one which has obviously crossed the minds of men since the very beginning of time. Death is inevitable. Death is inescapable. Thus, the significance of that question, "If a man die shall he live again?"

Men are still asking Job's question: the rich and the poor; the educated and the illiterate; the young and the old. All seek an answer to that question. And the Christian faith still provides an answer—the only answer—to that question.

Job asked, "If a man die shall he live again?" Jesus answered, "I am the resurrection and the life, he that believeth in me though he were dead, yet shall he live and whosoever liveth and believeth in me shall never die. Believest thou this?" (John 11:25-26). And Christians down through the centuries of time have affirmed it as stated in the Apostle's Creed, "I believe in the life everlasting."

Every earnest Christian has this same realization of sin and this same desire for moral and spiritual perfection. We, too, look for a life beyond the grave where our deepest moral and spiritual aspirations will at last be fulfilled. As the apostle John put it, "We know that when He shall appear that we shall be like Him, for we shall see Him as He is" (1 John 3:2b).

And, thus, the fact that man's destiny is unfulfilled in this life is itself evidence of a better life beyond the grave. Henry Wadsworth Longfellow has expressed it so well in "A Psalm of Life":

Tell me not in mournful numbers
Life is but an empty dream;
That the soul is dead that slumbers,
That things are not what they seem.

No, life is real, life is earnest
And the grave is not its goal.
Dust to dust and dust returneth,
Was not written of the soul.

INTELLIGENT DESIGN

When I consider your heavens, the work of your fingers, the moon and the stars, which you have set in place, what is man that you are mindful of him, the son of man that you care for him?

—Psalm 8:3-4 NIV

A group of young army officers was having a discussion about religion, a common topic in army "bull sessions." One young lieutenant said, "Until someone can prove to me scientifically the existence of God, I will not believe."

Just as he spoke the words the regimental chaplain entered the room. The young officer apologized, "Sorry, Chaplain."

The chaplain replied, "That's alright. I have a similar problem. Until someone can prove to me theologically the existence of an atom, I will not believe."

"Whoever heard of proving the existence of an atom theologically," protested the young officer.

"Exactly," said the chaplain.

Those engaged in the creation science versus evolutionary theory controversy should consider the possibility that they are speaking two different languages. Perhaps that would lead to a better understanding of the issue by both parties. In fact, one prominent scientist said that one of the reasons he became a believer is because of the remarkable correspondence between what he knew about the origin of the universe and Genesis 1 where the creation story is told.

Someone has said that Psalm 8 is Genesis 1 set to music. "When I consider your heavens, the work of your fingers, the moon and the stars, which you have set in place, what is man that you are mindful of him, the son of man that you care for him? You made him a little lower than the heavenly beings and crowned him with glory and honor. You made him ruler over the works of your hands" (Psalm 8:3-6 NIV).

IN THE PRESENCE OF MY ENEMY

You prepare a table before me in the presence of my enemies.
—Psalm 23:5a

During Operation Nordwind, the German counteroffensive in Eastern France in January 1945, my friend and I became separated from the rest of our company. In attempting to locate our unit we passed through a French village. We had not eaten or slept in twenty-four hours, so we knocked on the door of a home in the village and asked for food. A middle-aged couple invited us in and gave us some chicken soup. When we had finished with the meal, we asked if we could lie down and catch up on our sleep. The gentleman took us to an upstairs bedroom and indicated that we could rest there. The husband pointed to a photograph on the wall and told us it was his son, a nineteen or twenty year old like ourselves, but dressed in a German army uniform! Perhaps, as the couple showed us such hospitality, they were hoping that their son might be shown such kindness if found himself in a similar situation.

Later, as I thought about that incident, I remembered the words of the Twenty-third Psalm, "You prepare a table before me in the presence of my enemies" (v.5a). I had seen that promise fulfilled. I believe the other promises of the psalm to be true, "Surely, goodness and mercy shall follow me all the days of my life and I shall dwell in the house of the Lord forever" (v. 6).

GROWING OLD GRACEFULLY

The days of our lives are seventy years; and if by reason of strength they are eighty years, yet their boast is only labor and sorrow; for it is soon cut off, and we fly away.

—Psalm 90:10 NKJV

Back in the early fifties when I was serving my first church in Rockford, Illinois, one of my seminary classmates invited me to be the guest preacher for a week of meetings at his church, Judson Memorial Baptist in Joliet, Illinois. The meetings were to start on Sunday morning and conclude the following Sunday evening. The pastor suggested that since I did not know the people and they did not know me, it might be a good idea for me to teach the adult Sunday school class which met before the worship service. That way we could get better acquainted in a more informal setting.

That seemed like a good idea to me, so I agreed. I don't recall exactly what the lesson was about, but somehow we got on the subject of growing old. One of the middle-aged ladies in the class made an interesting comment. She said, "I think that people are like apples. The older they get the more mellow they become." What a beautiful thought! I should have left it there. I don't know whatever possessed me but I just blurted out the first thought that came into my head. I replied, "Yes, and some of them become just plain rotten."

That probably was not the most tactful thing to say to a group of people that you have just met, but it is true. I have spent a lot of time with elderly people and I have discovered that they tend to fall into two categories: the mellow and the rotten. In all fairness, let me say that does not apply only to senior citizens. For the adversities of life, whatever their nature, tend to make a person either better or bitter.

My contention is that you have a choice in the matter. For, you see, it doesn't make any difference how great the pressure is from the outside as long as the pressure from the inside is equal to it. One principle for growing old gracefully I learned from my Aunt Florence. This incident took place more that sixty-five years ago. The fact that I still remember it says something, I think, about its importance in my life. My aunt and her daughter, Norma, were having a discussion about the injustice of life. Norma and I were in high school at the time. Norma said, "Life isn't fair. You work hard all your life to earn enough money to enjoy life and then when you get enough money you are too old to enjoy it." I will never forget the answer of Aunt Florence. She replied, "Well, dear, you just have to learn to enjoy the struggle." That is the second principle for growing old gracefully. You just have to learn to enjoy the struggle.

That, too, is a biblical principle. In the first chapter of the book of James there is a beautiful sentence which affirms this principle. In the Phillips translation it reads, "When all kinds of trials and temptations crowd into your lives, my brothers, don't resent them as intruders, but welcome them as friends!" And then James goes on to explain, "Realize that they come to test your faith and to produce in you the quality of endurance."

There is an old Swedish hymn that expresses it so well:

Thanks for prayers that Thou hast answered, Thanks for what Thou dost deny!
Thanks for storms that I have weather, Thanks for all Thou does supply1
Thanks for pain and thanks for pleasure, Thanks for comfort in despair!
Thanks for grace that none can measure, Thanks for love beyond compare!

(A. L. Storm, "Thanks to God")

THE TRUSTING HEART

Trust in the Lord with all your heart and lean not on your own under-standing; in all your ways acknowledge Him, and He will make your paths straight.

—Proverbs 3:5-6 NIV

If there is one phrase which adequately describes a saint of God it is *a trusting heart*. A trusting heart is one which seeks to know God's will. For Proverbs 3:5 reads, "Trust in the Lord with *all* thine heart and lean not on your own understanding." If we are to know God's will we must have a complete regard for God's will. The first part of verse 5 says, "Trust in the Lord with *all* thine heart." And God has said, "Ye shall seek me and find me when ye search for me with all your heart" (Jer. 29:13).

A second characteristic of the trusting heart is that it seeks to do God's will. For in verse 6 we read, "In all thy ways acknowledge Him and He shall direct thy paths." And so then we must seek to do God's will.

One of the best examples of a trusting heart is George Beverly Shea, America's beloved gospel singer. After Mr. Shea had completed his training in sacred music, he sought a place in full-time Christian service but found none. And so he went to work in a New York City business office where he remained for nine years seeking the will of God. During this time he received a very attractive offer from a secular concern to sing popular music over a national network. And though Mr. Shea wanted to make music his career, he spurned the offer because he wanted to acknowledge God in all his ways. A short time later he was asked by the Club Aluminum Company to sing for them over the ABC network. This time he was asked to sing sacred music and so accepted. After nine years of waiting and testing he had found God's will. The first song which Mr. Shea sang on his program was more than his theme song. It was the theme of his life.

> The trusting heart to Jesus clings
> Nor any ill forebodes,
> But at the cross of Calvary sings
> Praise God for lifted loads.
>
> (Eliza E. Hewitt, "Singing I Go")

FAITH IS

Rejoice in the Lord always. I will say it again: Rejoice!
—Philippians 4:4

Pamela Reeve has published a colorful little booklet entitled *Faith Is...* It is patterned after the cartoon strip *Love Is...* except that in this case there are no pictures.

The booklet simply consists of a series of homey definitions and descriptions of faith. Let me share a few of those with you.

> "Faith is the handle by which I take God's promises and apply them to my particular problems."
>
> "Faith is doing the right thing regardless of the consequences, knowing God will turn the ultimate effect to good."
>
> "Faith is expecting God to accomplish miracles through insignificant me with my two fishes and five loaves."
>
> "Faith is confidence in God's faithfulness to me in an uncertain world on an uncharted course through an unknown future."

The definition that I like best is the one that says, "Faith is simply taking God at His word."

There is a very beautiful story about Hudson Taylor, famous missionary to China and founder of the China Inland Mission, which was once the largest missionary society in the world. Dr. Taylor served as general director of the society for over forty years and in all of that time never asked anyone to contribute to the work of China Inland Mission. Can you imagine? A preacher who never asked for money. He just prayed and God supplied the funds. On one occasion a secretary came to Dr. Taylor to report that there was only twenty-five cents left in the mission treasury. When you remember that Dr. Taylor was responsible for the salaries of hundreds of missionaries, that could be a very serious situation. But he simply replied, "How wonderful! Twenty-five cents and all the promises of God." So no matter how great the difficulties are that you face in your life, remember that you have all the promises of God.

THE FEAR OF GOD

Since you call on a Father who judges each man's work impartially, live your lives as strangers here in reverent fear.

—1 Peter 1:17 NIV

"The Fear of God" is a theme that occurs frequently throughout the Bible. As a matter of fact, that expression is found more than one hundred times in the Bible, mostly in the Old Testament. Nevertheless, it is a topic rarely proclaimed from the pulpits of our land. In the multi-volume encyclopedia *Twenty Centuries of Great Preaching* there is no sermon on the fear of God. Perhaps the reason for that is our misunderstanding of the meaning of fear, particularly in relation to Christian faith. An old sea captain put it this way: "I love the sea, but I also fear the sea." John Newton, who had been a sea captain before his conversion to Christ, wrote this in his best loved hymn "Amazing Grace":

'Twas grace that taught my heart to fear;
And grace my fear relieved.

The dictionary offers two definitions of fear: (1) dread, terror; (2) reverence, respect. The phrase "the Fear of God" is found just five times in the New Testament. Those five instances help us to see how the grace of God uses even the fear of God to do His work.

1. The fear of God distinguishes believers from unbelievers. "There is no fear of God before their eyes" (Rom. 3:18).
2. The fear of God prepares us for the judgment of God. "And if you call on the Father, who without respect of persons judgeth according to every man's work, pass the time of your sojourning here in fear" (1 Peter 1:17).

275

3. The fear of God motivates us to strive for perfection. "Having therefore these promises, dearly beloved, let us cleanse ourselves from all filthiness of the flesh and spirit, perfecting holiness in the fear of God" (2 Cor. 7:1).

4. The fear of God is the basis of Christian evangelism. "Since, then, we know what it is to fear the Lord, we try to persuade men. What we are is plain to God, and I hope it is also plain to your conscience" (2 Cor. 5:11 NIV).

5. The fear of God enables the church to grow in numbers. "Then the church throughout Judea, Galilee and Samaria enjoyed a time of peace. It was strengthened; and encouraged by the Holy Spirit, it grew in numbers, living in the fear of the Lord" (Acts 9:31 NIV).

LEAD US NOT INTO TEMPTATION

When words are many, sin is not absent; but he who holds his tongue is wise.

—Proverbs 10:19

Anyone who watches the movie ads has to agree that there has been a decided decline in moral standards in the contemporary scene. I have been reminded of a story about Joe E. Brown, the big-mouthed comedian so popular in the thirties and forties. Joe was on a tour in the South Pacific entertaining the troops during World War II. On this occasion his warm-up act was another comedian who told a bunch of dirty jokes.

Then Joe came on stage. He didn't say anything but did a soft shoe routine and made faces featuring his famous big mouth. The audience broke out in wild applause. Then Joe said, "You see. You don't have to be dirty to be funny."

Someone has said that the difference between a politician and a statesman is that a politician looks forward to the next election while the statesman looks forward to the next generation. A similar case can be made for humor. Abraham Lincoln was a great statesman. He was also a great humorist.

Yield not to temptation, for yielding is sin,
Each vict'ry will help you some other to win;
Fight manfully onward, dark passions subdue,
Look ever to Jesus, He will carry you through.

Shun evil companions, bad language disdain,
God's name hold in rev'rence, Nor take it in vain;
Be thoughtful and earnest, kind-hearted and true,
Look ever to Jesus, He will carry you through.
(Horatio R. Palmer, "Yield Not To Temptation")

THE MESSAGE OF THE CROSS: REDEMPTION

Jesus says: "And ye shall know the truth, and the truth shall make you free."

—John 8:32

Redemption is one of the greatest words of the Bible. It is, as a matter of fact, the theme of the Bible. We find it in the first book of the Bible, Genesis, on the dying lips of Joseph the patriarch. We find it in the last book of the Bible, Revelation, on the lips of men and angels gathered around the throne of God to sing His praises. We find the word or the idea of redemption in every book in between Genesis and Revelation. It is, in a very real sense, the theme of the Bible.

The word redemption, of course, is from the word *redeem.* If you look up the word *redeem* in the dictionary you will find this definition: "to buy back; to purchase." There is also a special theological definition in the dictionary which will help us to understand how the word is used in the Bible: "in theology, to deliver from sin and its penalties, as by a sacrifice made for the sinner."

Now there are several Greek words which are translated by our English word *redeem*, but there is one that is of special interest because it contains a word picture of what the Bible means when it speaks of redemption. It is a Greek word which is made up of two other Greek words, one which means "out of" and the other which means "marketplace." So this word, which is always translated "redeem" in the English New Testament, literally means "out of the marketplace." That word has special significance for our understanding of the New Testament concept of redemption because you see, the marketplace is where slaves were bought and sold. Therefore, to be redeemed is to be freed from slavery. The gospel is the sinner's Emancipation Proclamation. For it is the gospel of Christ that frees us from the penalty and power of sin.

As Jesus said, "If the Son therefore shall make you free, ye shall be free indeed" (John 8:36).

As you may know, it has been only in fairly recent times that debtor's prisons have ceased to exist. Once when Sylvia and I were in England we visited a lovely museum in York which had once been a debtor's prison. When General James Oglethorpe came to America to colonize Georgia, he went to the debtor's prisons of England and offered to pay the debts of such men if they would follow him to America. It was to such men that John Wesley ministered in his service in Georgia. Doubtless the Wesleys saw in James Oglethorpe a picture of our Lord and Savior Jesus Christ who redeemed us from the prison house of sin. It must have been that experience which caused Charles Wesley to write "O for a Thousand Tongues."

O for a thousand tongues to sing my great redeemer's praise;
The glories of my God and King, the triumphs of His grace.

He breaks the power of canceled sin, He sets the prisoner free;
His blood can make the foulest clean, His blood availed for me.

THE POWER OF THE RESURRECTION

For the message of the cross is foolishness to those who are perishing, but to us who are being saved it is the power of God.

—1 Corinthians 1:18 NIV

Dr. Robert Speer, the great missionary statesman, wrote this in one of his many books about our Lord Jesus Christ:

I believe there is no fact in history better attested than our Lord's resurrection. It rests upon evidence stronger than any evidence we have of any other event—as strong as the evidence of what took place on July 4, 1776. I believe we can rest as securely on the evidence of the resurrection as we can on the evidence that there is a Declaration of Independence. You say we have the document here and now. I say, men saw Him rise. You say, there is a nation living whose existence testifies to the Declaration of Independence. I say, there is a Kingdom of Christ in existence that bears witness to the fact that something lifted it out of death when he hung on the cross. It was saved by nothing less than His rising again from the dead. You say, the historic evidence does not satisfy everyone. I say, it convinces all who would be convinced as if they were to see Him risen with their own eyes.

There is a Kingdom of Christ that bears witness to the fact that something lifted it out of death when He hung on the cross. It was saved by nothing less than His rising again from the dead. We see evidence of that miraculous transformation in the sixteenth chapter of Mark. There can be no doubt that the death of Christ left the disciples in defeat, doubt, and despair. The women came to the tomb to embalm a dead body—not to worship a risen Savior. When the angel appeared and announced the resurrection to the women we read, "and they went out quickly, and fled from the sepulcher, for they trembled and were amazed; neither said they anything to any man; for they were afraid" (v. 8).

He first appeared to Mary Magdalene, out of whom He had cast seven devils. When she told the mourning disciples, "they, when they had heard that He was alive, and had been seen of her, believed not" (v. 11). "After that He appeared in another form unto two of them, as they walked, and went into the country. And they went and told it unto the others; neither believed they them" (vv. 12-13). "Afterwards He appeared unto the eleven as they sat at meat, and upbraided them with their unbelief and hardness of heart, because they believed not them which had seen Him after He was risen" (v. 14).

Gradually, the truth of what really happened dawned upon them and they believed. For, in the last verse of Mark's Gospel we read, "And they went forth, and preached everywhere, the Lord working with them, and confirming the word with signs following" (v. 20).

In the great city of Boston in the courtyard of the Old Trinity Church there is a huge statue of Phillips Brooks, the great American preacher who lived in the nineteenth century. Brooks stands there with an open Bible in his hand as though preaching to the crowds of people passing by. Standing beside him and slightly behind is the figure of Christ. That is the source of power in Brooks' preaching. It is also the source of the power of Moody and Spurgeon and Luther. The Lord working with them. Something lifted the kingdom out of death when He hung on the cross. It was saved by nothing less than His rising from the dead.

REACTIONS TO THE RESURRECTION

And if Christ is not risen, your faith is futile; you are still in your sins!
—1 Corinthians 15:17 NKJV

One of my seminary classmates had been converted to Christ in his senior year in the College of Engineering at Purdue University. He was enrolled that year in a course entitled "Speech for Engineers." When it came time for him to give his required speech before the class, he decided to share his newfound faith with his classmates. It was just before Easter, so he spoke for five minutes on the topic "Why I Believe in the Resurrection of Jesus Christ." His was the last speech of the day. When the teacher stood up to make assignments for the next class, one of the students raised his hand and said, "Please, let's not hear any more about the Easter bunny."

When the apostle Paul preached about Jesus and the resurrection to the philosophers in Athens he got a similar response from some in his audience. In Acts 17:32 Luke writes, "When they heard of the resurrection of the dead, some mocked." However, Luke also notes that some of them joined Paul and became believers.

It is quite clear that belief in the resurrection of Christ is the very cornerstone of the Christian faith. The subject of apostolic preaching was always Jesus and His resurrection. Paul said to the Corinthians, "If Christ is not risen, your faith is futile; you are still in your sins" (1 Cor. 15:17). To the Romans he wrote, "If you confess with your mouth the Lord Jesus and believe in your heart that God has raised Him from the dead, you will be saved" (10:9 NKJV).

He is Lord! He is Lord! He is risen from the dead and He is Lord! Every knee shall bow, every tongue confess that Jesus Christ is Lord! (traditional refrain)

283

ROCKET SCIENCE

So also is the resurrection of the dead. The body is sown in corruption, it is raised in incorruption.

—1 Corinthians 15:42 NKJV

Some few years ago in an article in the *New York Herald Tribune*, Dr. Wernher von Braun, the famous rocket scientist, discussed the subject of immortality. He said, "Science has found that nothing can disappear without a trace. Nature does not know extinction. All it knows is transformation. Now if God applies this fundamental principle to the most minute and insignificant parts of His universe, doesn't it make sense to assume that He applies it also to the masterpiece of His creation—the Human Soul? I think it does. And everything that science has taught me—and continues to teach me—strengthens my belief in the continuity of our spiritual existence after death."

This analogy between the new life that comes from death in nature and the immortality of the soul and the resurrection of the body is the very one that Paul uses in 1 Corinthians 15, the great resurrection chapter of the Bible. As he attempts to explain the nature of the resurrection body to the Christians at Corinth, he uses this same thought, "But some man will say, 'How are the dead raised up? And with what body do they come?' Thou fool, that which thou sowest is not quickened except it die; and that which thou sowest, thou sowest not that body that shall be, but bare grain, it may chance of wheat, or of some other grain, but God giveth it a body as it hath pleased him, and to every seed his own body....So also is the resurrection of the dead. It is sown in corruption, it is raised in incorruption; it is sown in dishonor, it is raised in glory; it is sown in weakness, it is raised in power; it is sown a natural body, it is raised a spiritual body" (1 Cor. 15:35-38, 42-44). And thus Paul concludes that creation itself gives evidence that there is a life beyond the grave.

For the beauty of the earth, for the glory of the skies,
For the love which from our birth over and around us lies
Lord of all to thee we raise this our hymn of grateful praise.

For the joy of human love, brother, sister, parent, child,
Friends on earth, and friends above, for all gentle thoughts and
    mild,
Lord of all, to Thee we raise this our hymn of grateful praise.
                    (Folliott S. Pierpoint, "For the Beauty of the Earth")

THE ARM OF GOD

He tends His flock like a shepherd: He gathers the lambs in His arms and
carries them close to His heart; He gently leads those that have young.
—Isaiah 40:11 NIV

One of the most interesting things about the Old Testament is the
fact that although the children of Israel were forbidden to worship God
with images, their sacred writings are filled with imagery. The second
commandment forbade the people to make any image of God of wood,
stone, or precious metal. God was not to be represented in any earthly,
human form.

Nevertheless, there are many poetic expressions in the Old
Testament which ascribe to God human and earthly characteristics.
These metaphors, for the most part, are like the parables of Jesus in
that they are earthly expressions with heavenly meanings. These are
so frequent in the Old Testament that it is not difficult to call several
of them to mind. For example, in Proverbs we are told that "The eyes
of the Lord are every place beholding the evil and the good" (15:3).
The psalmist prays, "Incline thine ear unto me, O Lord, and hear my
speech" (17:6). And Ezra, having led the children of Israel out of the
Babylonian captivity, cries, "The good hand of our God was upon us"
(Ezra 8:18a).

One of the most interesting expressions of this kind, it seems to
me, is that expression "the arm of God." It is a favorite of Isaiah. As a
matter of fact, he uses that expression more frequently than any other
writer in the Bible. And it occurs twice in Isaiah 40, one of the most
beautiful chapters in all the Bible. Here God is saying to His people, to
you and to me, "You who are weary, worn, and wounded, lean upon
the arm of the Lord."

On one occasion, a Sunday school teacher was teaching her class of
girls from Matthew 11 and quoted the words of Jesus, "Take my yoke

upon you." And she asked the girls, "What is a yoke?" One of them replied, "That is something that you put around the necks of animals." And the teacher asked, "What, then, is God's yoke?" There was silence for a minute and then one little girl raised her hand and said, "Well, God's yoke is when Jesus puts his arms around us." And so it is. "For He shall feed His flock like a shepherd: He shall gather the lambs with his arm, and carry them in His bosom" (Isaiah 40:11).

THE FRIEND OF GOD

And the scripture was fulfilled which saith, Abraham believed God, and it was imputed unto him for righteousness; and he was called the Friend of God.

—James 2:23

In three different portions of Scripture this great patriarch, Abraham, the Father of the Hebrew Nation, is called the Friend of God. He is called the Friend of God in 2 Chronicles, in the Book of Isaiah, and in the Epistle of James. Abraham was indeed the Friend of God.

There is a persistent question that continually reasserts itself whenever I think of Abraham, the Friend of God. And that is, Why is Abraham called the Friend of God? Why of all the great men of the Bible is just this one man given that title? Why not David, the man after God's own heart? Or Moses the servant of the Lord? Or John, the disciple whom Jesus loved? Why is Abraham alone called the Friend of God?

The Bible says that a friend loves at all times. If Abraham was the Friend of God, then he must have loved God at all times. And this, of course, was true of Abraham. Here was a man who, because of his great love for God, left his home in Ur of the Chaldees to venture forth and possess a land that God had promised him. Here was a man who loved God so much that he was willing to offer his only son at God's command. Truly, Abraham loved God at all times.

And the Friend of God sticks close to God. The Bible says, "A friend sticketh closer than a brother" (Prov. 18:24b). And this Abraham did, for on several occasions God appeared to Abraham to renew this covenant of friendship. Abraham was faithful in his end of the bargain, for he cultivated a closeness to God. Wherever he went in his wanderings he always remembered to build an altar to his God.

And finally, the friend of God obeys the commands of God. Jesus said to His disciples on that occasion in the upper room, "You are My friends if you do whatever I command you" (John 15:14 NKJV). Does this sound strange? Do friends command each other? Yes, for you see to a friend, the slightest wish is an urgent command. And this made Abraham the friend of God. For God had only to indicate His desire and Abraham was willing to sacrifice everything to please God. This brings us back to Jesus' great commandment: "Thou shalt love the Lord thy God" (Matt. 22:37). That is not really a commandment, because you cannot command love. "But we love Him [God] because He first loved us." And therefore we seek to obey His commands and do those things which are pleasing in His sight.

> What a friend we have in Jesus, all our sins and griefs to bear!
> What a privilege to carry everything to God in prayer!
> O what peace we often forfeit, O what needless pain we bear,
> All because we do not carry everything to God in prayer!
> (Joseph Scriven, "What a Friend We Have in Jesus")

THE GOOD SHEPHERD

I am the Good Shepherd. The Good Shepherd lays down His life for the sheep.

—John 10:11 NIV

The tenth chapter of the Gospel of John is the Twenty-third Psalm of the New Testament. In Psalm 23 David said, "The Lord is my shepherd." Here Jesus says, "I am the Good Shepherd." In the New Testament Jesus is described as the Good Shepherd, the Great Shepherd, and the Chief Shepherd. Here in John 10, He refers to Himself twice as the Good Shepherd. In Hebrews 12:20 He is described as the Great Shepherd: "Now the God of peace that brought again from the dead our Lord Jesus, that Great Shepherd of the sheep, through the blood of the everlasting covenant, make you perfect in every good work to do His will, working in you that which is well pleasing in his sight." In his first epistle Peter speaks of Jesus when he says, "When the Chief Shepherd shall appear you shall receive a crown of glory that does not fade away" (1 Peter 5:4). Christians today can say, "The Lord Jesus Christ is my Shepherd. I shall not want. We are His people and the sheep of His pasture."

There was an interesting article in the *Reader's Digest* some time ago entitled "The Basque Sheepherder and the Twenty-Third Psalm." The Basques live in Spain and are the most famous sheep men in the world. At one point in the article the shepherd describes the loving relationship that exists between the sheep and his shepherd.

In the Holy land each sheep takes his place in the grazing line in the morning and keeps the same position throughout the day. Once during the day, however, each sheep leaves its place and goes to the shepherd. Whereupon the shepherd stretches out his hand and rubs the animal's nose and ears, scratches its chin, whispers

291

affectionately to it. The sheep, meanwhile, nibbles at the shepherd's ear or rubs its cheek against his face. After a few minutes of this communion with the master, the sheep returns to its place in the feeding line.

We cultivate this kind of relationship with the Good Shepherd as we pray to Jesus, as we read His Word, worship Him together, and sing the great hymns of our faith.

THE LIGHT OF THE WORLD

I am the light of the world; he that follows me shall not walk in darkness, but shall have the light of life.

—*John 8:12*

These words in John 8:12 are the second of the "I am" sayings in the Gospel of John. There are seven in all. In chapter 6 we read, "I am the Bread of life." In chapter 10, "I am the Good Shepherd" and "I am the Door." In chapter 11, "I am the Resurrection and the Life." In chapter 14, "I am the Way, the Truth and the Life." And in chapter 15, "I am the True Vine."

These sayings are a conscious effort on the part of Jesus to identify with the Lord God Jehovah. When God appeared to Moses in the burning bush in the desert, Moses asked, "Who are you?" God replied, "I AM that I AM." That is, the self-existent one. When Moses asked, "Whom shall I tell Pharaoh has sent me?" God said, "Say that I AM has sent you." So when Jesus said "I am the Light of the World," He was claiming to be that same God.

These "I am" sayings are alike in that they have a similar structure. Each one has in it a claim, a promise, and a commandment implied or explicit. Here the claim is: "I am the Light of the World." The promise is: you shall not walk in darkness but shall have the light of life. The commandment is: follow me. So, you see, a Christian is one who accepts the claims of Christ, who believes the promises of Christ, and who obeys the commands of Christ.

There is a beautiful hymn with words by John Henry Newman written in a time of great personal struggle in his own life. May it ever be our prayer.

Lead kindly light, amid the encircling gloom lead Thou me on;
The night is dark, and I am far from home; lead Thou me on.
Keep Thou my feet; I do not ask to see
The distant scene; one step enough for me.

THE LIVING WATER

The Spirit and the bride say, "Come!" And let him who hears say, "Come!" Whoever is thirsty, let him come; and whoever wishes, let him take the free gift of the water of life.

—Revelation 22:17

The incident of the Samaritan woman at the well is a parable as well as a miracle. It is an earthly story with a heavenly meaning. A parable is a comparison. In this passage of Scripture we find that Jesus' physical thirst provides the occasion for Him to talk to this woman about her spiritual thirst. Although this was an actual historical incident in the life of Jesus, it is nevertheless the parable of the living water.

This comparison is one that occurs many places in Scripture. The psalmist writes, "As the deer pants after the water brooks, so pants my soul after Thee, O God. My soul thirsts for God" (Psalm 42:2). The prophet Isaiah invites people to find God with these words: "Ho, everyone that is thirsty, come to the waters" (Isa. 55:1). God's final invitation to man in the book of Revelation is stated in these terms: "The Spirit and the bride say, Come. And let him that heareth say, Come. And let him that is athirst come. And whosoever will, let him take the water of life freely" (Rev. 22:17). The great message of God in these things is simply this: when you desire God as much as a man dying of thirst desires water, you will find Him.

I think of the life of James Chalmers, a great missionary from Scotland to New Guinea where he established 130 preaching stations before he was killed by cannibals. He was a great witness for Christ to both small and great. Robert Louis Stevenson said of James Chalmers, "He is the most attractive, simple, brave and interesting man in the whole Pacific."

It all began back in Inverary, Scotland, when a team of Irish evangelists came to the area. Chalmers and his friends decided that they were going to break the meetings up and send the evangelists packing off to Ireland. But a Christian friend persuaded Chalmers that he ought not to do this until he had heard the men and had a chance to judge for himself. So Chalmers borrowed his friend's Bible and went off to the meeting. That night the youngest of the evangelists was the preacher. He took as his text the great words of Revelation, "The Spirit and the bride say, Come. And let him that heareth say, Come. And let him that is athirst come. And whosoever will, let him take the water of life freely." God spoke to the heart of Chalmers and years later he described his experience that night in this way: "I was athirst and I came." And that is what it means to be a Christian and a Christian witness, simply to be able to say "I was athirst and I came."

> I heard the voice of Jesus say, "Behold, I freely give
> The living water; thirsty one, stoop down, and drink and live."
> I came to Jesus, and I drank of that life-giving stream;
> My thirst was quenched, my soul revived, and now I live in Him.
> (Horatius Bonar, "I Heard the Voice of Jesus Say")

THE LIVING WORD

In the beginning was the Word, and the Word was with God, and the Word was God.

—John 1:1

In one scene from Goethe's *Faust*, that immortal classic of world literature, we see Faust, a philosopher and theologian, alone in his study. He has nothing with which to occupy his mind and so, wishing to pass the time away, he turns to his New Testament to translate from the original Greek to his native German. The passage that he selects is this portion of John's Gospel. He begins, "In the beginning was the Word." Then he changes his translation in turn to "In the beginning was the thought," "In the beginning was the power," "In the beginning was the act."

Finally, the great scholar concludes that if he is to render the thought of this passage, he must be taught by the Spirit of God. It should not surprise us that the brilliant Dr. Faust was confounded by these words. For here on the most profound page of the most profound book known to humankind, we find the most profound thought, and that is that when Jesus was born in Bethlehem, God assumed human form. If you compare John 1:1 with verse 14 you see that very plainly: "In the beginning was the Word and the Word was with God and the Word was God" (v. 1); "And the Word was made flesh and dwelt among us" (v. 14a). As John says in his first epistle, "Our eyes have seen, our ears have heard and our hands have handled the Word of Life" (1 John 1:1).

Dr. A. J. Gordon, pastor and founder of Gordon College and Seminary, once told of an experience that brought these things home to him. One day during the Christmas season, he was looking in a store window. A little boy came up beside him and also looked in the window. Then the boy looked up and saw Dr. Gordon's beard. His curiosity was aroused since beards were not then in style. Finally the little boy got up enough courage to ask, "Say, mister, are you Jesus?" Dr. Gordon was a little startled by the question but he assured the boy that he was not Jesus. Then he talked to him about the real Jesus and they went their separate ways. Dr. Gordon said that all through that week the little boy's question kept ringing in his ears, "Say, mister, are you Jesus?" He kept asking himself, "Do people really see Jesus living in me?" That is the question that every Christian must continually ask, for the world will receive this Savior when they see Him living in us.

THE ASCENSION OF OUR LORD

Now when He had spoken these things, while they watched, He was taken up, and a cloud received Him out of their sight.

—Acts 1:9 NKJV

Ascension Day is the day when we celebrate our Savior's return to heaven. The ascension of our Lord is described in the very simplest terms in three passages in the New Testament. In the closing words of Mark's Gospel we are told, "So then, after the Lord had spoken unto them, he was received up into heaven, and sat on the right hand of God" (Mark 16:19). In the parallel passage in Luke we read, "And it came to pass, while he blessed them, he was parted from them, and carried up into heaven" (Luke 24:51). And in Acts 1:9, "And when he had spoken these things, while they beheld, he was taken up; and a cloud received him out of their sight."

In addition to these brief descriptions of the ascension of our Lord, however, there are many other references to the event throughout the New Testament. As a matter of fact, every writer of the New Testament alludes to the ascension of our Lord. For the ascension is not only a great fact of the New Testament, but it is also a great factor in the life of Christ and in the Christian life. No complete view of Jesus Christ is possible unless the ascension and its consequences are included. It is the consummation of His redemptive work. The Christ of the Gospels is the Christ of history, the Christ of the past; but the full New Testament picture of Christ is that of a living Christ, the Christ of heaven, the Christ of experience, the Christ of the present and the future. That is the message of the ascension.

Reviewing all the teaching of our Lord's present life in heaven—appearing on our behalf, interceding in God's presence, bestowing the Holy Spirit, governing and guiding the church, sympathizing, helping and saving His people—we are called upon to lift up our hearts. For it is in relation to the living Christ that we find the secret of peace, the assurance of access, and the guarantee of our permanent relation to God. The motto of every Christian in this time should be "Keep looking up."

THE RACE OF LIFE

I press on toward the goal to win the prize for which God has called me heavenward in Christ Jesus.

—*Philippians 3:14 NIV*

In several passages in the New Testament life is described as a race to be run. To the Christians at Corinth Paul says, "Know you not that they which run in a race run all, but one receives the prize? So run that you may obtain" (1 Cor. 9:24). The writer of the Epistle to the Hebrews exhorts, "Let us lay aside every weight and the sin which does so easily beset us and let us run with patience the race that is set before us looking unto Jesus, the Author and Finisher of our Faith" (12:2).

Perhaps the most significant passage of this kind is found in Philippians 3:13-14 where the apostle Paul outlines his strategy for winning the race of life: "This one thing I do; forgetting those things which are behind, and reaching forth unto those things which are before, I press toward the mark for the prize of the high calling of God in Christ Jesus."

Some years ago now it was my privilege to attend a youth rally addressed by Gil Dodds, the Flying Parson. He was called the Flying Parson because while he was still a student at what is now Gordon-Conwell Divinity School, he broke the world's record for the indoor one-mile run. In his talk Gil Dodds told of a conversation which he had with Glen Cunningham, another famous miler. It was Glen Cunningham's record that Dodds broke. In their conversation Cunningham described the race at Dartmouth where he had set the record for the indoor one-mile run. He came within a few seconds of being the first person to run a four minute mile. He said to Gil Dodds, "The only reason that I didn't run a four minute mile that night is because I had made up my mind that it couldn't be done."

Although Gil Dodds didn't run a four minute mile either, he did break Cunningham's record. After the race where he broke the record a reporter asked this great Christian athlete, "Gil, to what do you attribute your success tonight?"

Without a moment's hesitation Dodds replied in the words of the apostle Paul, "I can do all things through Christ who strengthens me."

So, then, toe the mark. Get set. Run the race of life. There's a prize awaiting you.

THE TRUE VINE

I am the vine; you are the branches. If a man remains in me and I in him, he will bear much fruit; apart from me you can do nothing.
—John 15:5 NIV

In the May 1977 issue *of Reader's Digest,* Alex Haley answered some of the many questions about his best-selling novel *Roots* in an article entitled "What Roots Means to Me." In the first paragraph he writes, "I am sometimes asked to explain the success of *Roots,* to pinpoint what it is that this book has touched, and the answer is really very simple. In all of us there is a hunger, marrow-deep, to know our heritage—to know who we are and where we have come from." Most of us would acknowledge a basic human need to belong to others and to identify with them.

Although this is obviously true of human and temporal relationships, it is even more true of divine and eternal ones. As the poet has said, "My one unchanged obsession wheresoe'er my feet have trod is a deep, abiding, never sated thirst for God."

It is these matters that are the subject of the parable of the vine and the branches. For as Jesus celebrated the Passover feast in the upper room with His disciples, He suddenly announced that He was going to leave them. He had tried to prepare them for His death, but somehow they did not comprehend. Their hearts were filled with doubt and fear. What will become of the Kingdom and of us? Who will lead us?

Every attempt to quiet their fears somehow falls on deaf ears. But now as He walks with his disciples from the upper room to Gethsemane, Jesus seizes upon this allegory—the parable of the vine and the branches—to make plain to them what was otherwise obscure: the reality of his spiritual presence.

It is this same presence that is the source of strength, hope, and courage to bewildered and struggling disciples today. He has said to us,

"I will never leave you nor forsake you. Lo, I am with you always even unto the end of the world."

It is this great truth that changed the life of John Wesley. One day on a ship on the Atlantic Ocean one of the Moravian brethren asked Wesley, "Do you know Jesus Christ as your Savior?"

Wesley replied, "I know that Jesus Christ is the Savior of the world."

"But," said the Moravian, "is He your Savior?"

Although Wesley replied in the affirmative, he wrote in his diary, "I fear my answer was vain." But there came that day at a meeting in a house on Aldersgate Street in London, when listening to one reading from Luther's commentary on the Epistle to the Romans, he felt his heart strangely warmed. He had experienced personal faith in Jesus Christ.

THE GREAT PHYSICIAN

Is there no balm in Gilead? Is there no physician there?
—Jeremiah 8:22a NIV

In reading the Gospel of Mark it is important to understand the nature of miracles. For Mark is the gospel of miracles. Of the thirty-five miracles of our Savior that are described in detail in the four Gospels, nineteen of them are related in Mark's Gospel, which incidentally is the shortest book of the four. Miracles are of special importance to Mark and his readers.

The word that is most frequently used to denote miracles in the New Testament is "sign." Miracles have a meaning beyond their physical appearance. Every miracle is a parable. A parable is an earthly story with a heavenly meaning. The miracles are true stories. They really happened. But they have a higher meaning. For example, Jesus gives as the meaning of the healing of the paralytic in this passage, "that you may know that the Son of Man hath power on earth to forgive sins" (Matt. 9:6).

Let me tell you the story of a twentieth-century leper who was also a demoniac and a paralytic. He was a student at Roberts Wesleyan College. His name is Jose Valentine. Everybody called him Angel, Angel Valentine. He had not always been an angel. He was once a member of a Puerto Rican gang in the Bronx. He was a drug addict and a pusher. He supported his drug habit by burglary and robbery. Eventually he was arrested. While he was in jail someone spoke to him of Christ. He received Christ as his Savior and Lord and was delivered from drugs. He came to Rochester to enroll in a drug treatment program at Teen Challenge. He graduated from Roberts Wesleyan College, married a lovely nurse, and went on to graduate from Asbury Theological Seminary and is now serving as a pastor.

Several times while he was a student at Roberts, Angel spoke in the chapel service. No speaker ever held the attention of students as well as he did. It is simply amazing to think that such a humble, sincere, honest, kind man was once a drug addict and a street thug. Jesus Christ changed his life. And Jesus Christ can change your life. For the Scripture says, "If anyone is in Christ, he is a new creation; old things are passed away; behold, all things have become new" (2 Cor. 5:17 NKJV).

THE LAW AND THE GOSPEL

For what the law was powerless to do in that it was weakened by the sinful nature, God did by sending His own Son in the likeness of sinful man to be a sin offering. And so He condemned sin in sinful man, in order that the righteous requirements of the law might be fully met in us, who do not live according to the sinful nature but according to the Spirit.
—Romans 8:3-4 NIV

The world was at the point of war. The countdown had begun. Fingers were poised above the buttons that would set off the mutual destruction. This was the state of the world described in a parable by P. D. East, editor of *The Petal Papers*. But both camps hesitated. They knew that war would not leave one living thing on this planet. In a final desperate effort they agreed to call a truce for forty-eight hours.

Those forty-eight hours were devoted to a conference of all the learned men of the world, gathered from every discipline and every area of knowledge. They were provided with the most sophisticated computer which was able, given adequate material, to solve any problem correctly.

One by one these learned men shared their specialized knowledge with the computer, until it was provided with all that man had learned through the ages, from every field of human endeavor and from every aspect of life. Now fully informed, the machine was asked a series of questions.

How can we save the world?
How can we save ourselves? Our families?
How can we live in peace on this earth?

Slowly, ever so slowly, the brain began to print its answer, and the answer it gave was this: "I am the Lord your God. You shall have

307

no other gods before me. You shall not make any graven image. You shall not take God's name in vain. Remember the Sabbath day to keep it holy. Honor your father and your mother. You shall not kill. You shall not commit adultery. You shall not steal. You shall not bear false witness. You shall not covet anything that is your neighbor's" (Exod. 20:2-17). In the parable, however, the brain did not tell men how to keep the Ten Commandments.

This brings me to what I want to say: that is *what you must do.* That is, what you must do in order that the righteousness of the law might be fulfilled in you. Sanctification is the process of becoming righteous, as distinguished from justification which is being declared righteous. Sometimes justification is spoken of as a positional righteousness. We are in Christ, therefore we have the righteousness of Christ in the sight of God. Sanctification is sometimes called practical righteousness, which is the process of actually becoming righteous. Someone has called sanctification "the Christianizing of the Christian."

An illustration which has helped me to understand the difference between justification and sanctification is my military experience. In November 1943 I was inducted into the United States Army at Camp Dodge, Iowa. As soon as I was sworn in I was a soldier even though I hardly knew which end of the rifle the bullets came out. But in the eyes of the United States government I was a soldier just as much as General Eisenhower who had spent twenty-five years in the army. However, it took many months of training before I was really a soldier in any sense of the word.

ALMOST BUT NOT QUITE

I am Alpha and Omega, the beginning and the end, the first and the last.

—Revelation 22:13

In the old Temple Baptist Church in Rockford, Illinois, there is a beautiful stained glass window representation of these words from the book of Revelation: a full figure of Jesus with the letters alpha and omega at His feet. At least it was intended to be. Unfortunately, the workman who installed the window did not read Greek. The problem arose when it came to installing the panel containing the letter omega. Omega is the last letter of the Greek alphabet, so when Jesus says "I am Alpha and Omega" He is saying what we mean when we say something is everything from A to Z.

The difficulty arose because the Greek letter upsilon looks just like an upside-down omega. The workman assumed that the omega was a "U" and installed it that way. So instead of Jesus saying "I am Alpha and Omega," we have Jesus saying "I am Alpha and Upsilon." Upsilon is farther down the alphabet than omega. The omega was installed as an upsilon and remained in place seventy-five years until the building was sold.

There are a great many people who would have Jesus saying "I am Alpha and Upsilon." That is to say, they accept Jesus for less than He is. Some would say that He is a great social reformer but not the Son of God. Others would say that He was a great teacher but not the Son of God.

In the first century of Christian history, people in the Roman provinces were required to go to the regional administrative headquarters and proclaim, "Caesar is Lord." No Christian could do that. Many paid with their lives for their refusal. ***If being a Christian today was a crime, would there be enough evidence to convict you?***

AUTHOR OF LIBERTY

Proclaim liberty throughout the land to all its inhabitants.
—Leviticus 25:10b NIV

One of the most sacred symbols of democracy is the Liberty Bell, an emblem of American freedom. It is no mere coincidence that the Liberty Bell is graced with a biblical quotation, the words of Leviticus 25:10—"Proclaim liberty throughout the land unto all the inhabitants thereof." It is no mere coincidence, because the religious and political history of the American people is certainly intertwined. It is true that our founding fathers taught the separation of church and state. But they did not for one minute believe in the separation of God and government. Rather, they believed that our nation was founded by God and was totally dependent upon God for its continuing existence.

What our fathers believed about America, the author of Psalm 85 believed about his nation. This psalm was written during the time of Ezra and Nehemiah, after the return of the people of Israel from the Babylonian captivity. This great event in the nation's history the psalmist attributes to God. He says, "Lord, thou has been favorable unto thy land" (Psalm 85:1). He does not attribute this political good fortune to the generosity of Cyrus the Persian, who freed his people, but to the favor of God. And prior to the captivity the prophets did not teach that the captivity was a result of political developments, but rather they taught that it was the judgment of God upon a sinful nation. The history of Israel would teach any nation that righteousness exalteth a nation but that sin is a reproach to any people.

The history of our great nation and the teachings of the Bible would indicate that if we are to remain free from tyranny we must remain true to God. A liberty-loving people must be a God-fearing people.

Our fathers' God, to Thee,
Author of liberty,
To thee we sing;
Long may our land be bright
With freedom's holy light;
Protect us by Thy might,
Great God, our King!

(Samuel F. Smith, "My Country, 'Tis of Thee")

 NOT NO, BUT NOW

For a great and effective door has opened to me, and there are many adversaries.

—1 Corinthians 16:9 NKJV

Two men looked out of prison bars. One saw mud; the other saw stars. It is amazing that two people can look at the same scene and see quite different things. It was so with the children of Israel. After the exodus from Egypt twelve men were sent into Canaan, the Promised Land, to spy out the country. Ten returned and reported, "There are giants in the land." Joshua and Caleb saw it quite differently: "The land is flowing with milk and honey." Sometimes we fail to see God's plan when it is laid out before us.

Gretchen Wilson, in her book *Red Neck Woman,* tells of the first big break that launched her fabulous career in country music. She was singing her audition songs in front of John Grady, president of Sony Music. While she was singing, he sat behind his big desk. At one point she looked up and he was rummaging through his desk looking for something to write with and did not appear to be listening to her. She was sure that this was another rejection (number 9). She was even more sure when she saw what he had written—two letters, N and O. As she was leaving, he showed her the slip of paper. What he actually wrote was NOW, meaning sign her up now. So it is that sometimes when God seems to be saying *no* he is really saying *now.* "Now is the accepted time, behold now is the day of salvation" (2 Cor. 6:2b).

God moves in mysterious ways His wonders to perform;
He plants His footsteps in the sea, and rides upon the storm

REFLECTIONS OF A SOLDIER AND SERVANT

Deep in unfathomable mines of never failing skill
He treasures up His bright designs, and works His sovereign will.
(William Cowper)

CONFESSING CHRIST

*Whosoever therefore shall confess me before men, him will I confess also
before my Father which is in heaven. But whosoever shall deny me before
men, him will I also deny before my Father which is in heaven.*

—Matthew 10:32-33

Mark 8:27-38 has often been called "Peter's Great Confession."
It deserves to be called that because it contains the most forthright
affirmation of Jesus' Messiahship in the gospels, at least to this point in
Jesus' ministry. In response to Jesus' question "Who do you say that I
am?" Peter replies, "You are the Christ" (v. 29 NIV). Or as Matthew re-
cords it, "You are the Christ, the Son of the living God" (16:16 NIV).

Yet it was not Peter's greatest confession. We see Peter again with
our Lord standing beside the Sea of Galilee following the resurrection.
Peter had three times denied the Lord during those terrible days of
the trial and crucifixion of the Savior. The Lord forgives him and asks
Peter, "Do you love me?" Peter, in the confession of a forgiven sinner,
replies, "Yes, Lord, you know that I love you" (John 21:15-17). He had
once confessed Jesus as Messiah or Christ, and now he confesses Him
as Savior. This was an even greater confession.

Still, it was not Peter's greatest confession. For on the day of
Pentecost we see Peter standing before the multitude in Jerusalem
proclaiming, "Let all the house of Israel know assuredly, that God has
made that same Jesus, whom you have crucified, both Lord and Christ"
(Acts 2:6). Christ. Savior. Lord. That was Peter's greatest confession.
For as the apostle Paul said to the Philippian jailer, "Believe in the Lord
Jesus Christ and you will be saved" (Acts 16:31 NIV).

One of my seminary classmates, Louis Goldberg, was born into a
Jewish family. While a student in the College of Engineering at Purdue
University, he came to believe that Jesus was the Messiah and received
him as his Savior. He went back to Brooklyn to explain his decision to

his parents. They ordered him out of their home and told him that they never wanted to see him again. As he walked from his home to the bus stop in the Jewish section of Brooklyn where his parents lived, people who had heard of his conversion leaned out of their windows to shout curses at him. He paid a price to confess Christ but God rewarded him for his faith. He served for many years as professor of Old Testament at Moody Bible Institute.

THE MEANING OF FAITH

Now faith is being sure of what we hope for and certain of what we do not see.

—Hebrews 11:1 NIV

The author of the Epistle to the Hebrews begins this, the great faith chapter of the Bible, with a definition: "Now faith is the substance of things hoped for; the evidence of things not seen." Then he illustrates the meaning of faith from the lives of some of the great people in the Old Testament.

I would like to illustrate the meaning of faith from the life of one of these men—Abraham. I have chosen Abraham for several reasons. He is called by the adherents of three of the world's great religions—Hebrew, Christian, and Muslim—"the Father of the Faithful." When the apostle Paul, writing to the Christians at Rome about justification by faith, needs an illustration of faith, he chooses Abraham. When James, in his epistle, needs an illustration of the relationship between faith and works he, too, points to Abraham. Emerson said that, "History is but the lengthened shadow of great men." The history of personal faith is but the lengthened shadow of Abraham.

You will find no written expression of faith from Abraham as you have in the law of Moses or the psalms of David or the prophecies of Isaiah. Nevertheless, he is referred to more often in the New Testament than any of these. For his life speaks volumes and the message is always the same: "Have faith in God." From him we learn the meaning of faith.

*The life of Abraham teaches us that **faith is answering the call of God**.* In the twelfth chapter of the book of Genesis, where the story of Abraham begins we read, "Now the Lord had said unto Abram, Get thee out of your country, from your family, and from your father's house, to a land that I will show you" (v. 1). "So Abram departed as the LORD had spoken to him" (v. 3a NKJV).

Further, the life of Abraham teaches us that **faith is claiming the promises of God.** When God called Abraham in Ur, He said to him, "I will make of thee a great nation, and I will bless thee, and make thy name great; and I will bless them that bless thee"(Gen. 12:2). As a matter of fact, God repeated and expanded the promises to Abraham all the years of his life. He promised Abraham a country, a nationality, happiness, greatness, service, protection, and that he should be a blessing to others.

Finally, the life of Abraham teaches us that **faith is doing the will of God.** The apostle John writes, "He that doeth the will of God abideth forever" (1 John 2:17b). No man was ever more committed to the will of God than Abraham, who in response to the command of God was willing to sacrifice upon an altar his only son, the heir of promise. For by this time he had so learned to trust God as never to doubt his purpose. "Faith is the setting of the entire self Godward" (Bishop Dubose).

What, then, is faith? Faith is the substance of things hoped for; the evidence of things not seen (Heb. 11:1). "It is that feeling or faculty within us by which the future becomes to our minds greater than the present; and what we do not see more powerful to influence us than what we do see" (Thomas Arnold).

Faith says to the farmer "Sow your seed"; to the aviator, "Spread your wings"; to the miner, "Sink your shaft"; to the sailor, "Hoist your sail"; to the engineer, "Survey your bridge"; to the explorer, "Follow your dream"; and to the saint, "On your knees."

A BANNER FOR THE PEOPLE

In that day the Root of Jesse will stand as a banner for the peoples; the nations will rally to Him, and His place of rest will be glorious.
—Isaiah 11:10 NIV

In order to understand this passage of the book of Isaiah, it is necessary to have some understanding of the place of the Messianic hope in the history of Israel. The word *messiah* is, of course, a Hebrew word. It means "the anointed one." The Greek translation is *Christos* from which we get our English word *Christ*.

In ancient Israel, prophets, priests, and kings were anointed with oil as they assumed office, symbolizing God's blessing upon them. Over the centuries, the idea developed that someday there would appear in Israel one who would be prophet, priest, and king. He would be known not simply as a messiah, as were these others, but rather as *the* Messiah. That theme runs throughout the Old Testament. In fact, of the thirty-nine books in the Old Testament, thirty-seven have at least one reference to the Messiah. That is remarkable when we remember that those thirty-nine books were written over a period of nearly a thousand years.

One of the more interesting aspects of the study of the messianic idea is the descriptive titles given to this person throughout the Bible. There are three such titles in this passage from Isaiah 11. In verse 1 the Messiah is spoken of as a *Shoot from the stump of Jesse* and the *Branch*. Then, in verse 10 he is spoken of as a *Banner for the peoples*.

Now, the Hebrew word that is translated "banner" is also translated by the words "ensign" and "standard" in the King James Bible. It is a military term. In ancient times, generals did not have radios or telephones to keep in touch with their troops and so had to rely on other means to keep their troops together. Each military unit had its own distinctive banner or ensign. If, in the heat of battle, a soldier became separated from his unit he would look for this banner or ensign which was displayed on a long pole. He would know that is where he was supposed to be. That is why Isaiah writes of the Messiah in verse 10, "the nations will rally to Him."

As Christians we, of course, believe that Jesus Christ is the Messiah and therefore "the banner for the people." He is the one whom we look to for guidance and direction. He is the one who will lead us to victory.

> There's a royal banner given for display
> To the soldiers of the King;
> As an ensign fair we lift it up today,
> While as ransomed ones we sing.
>
> Marching on, marching on,
> For Christ count everything but loss!
> And to crown Him King, toil and sing
> 'Neath the banner of the cross!
>
> (Daniel W. Whittle, "The Banner of the Cross")

A MISSION STATEMENT

Therefore go and make disciples of all nations, baptizing them in the name of the Father and of the Son and of the Holy Spirit.
—Matthew 28:19

Every organization should have a mission statement. As someone has said, "If you don't know where you're going, you'll probably end up somewhere else." A mission statement should be specific in its objectives but general in regard to the means for reaching those objectives. A good example of such a mission statement is the order that General Eisenhower received when he was appointed Supreme Commander of the Allied Expeditionary Force. Although he would lead the largest and most complex military operation in the history of the world, his orders consisted of a single sentence which said essentially, "Enter the continent of Europe and destroy the ability of the enemy to wage war." The military planners then spent many months working out the details.

Before He left this earth, our Lord gave the church a mission statement: "Go into all the world and make disciples of all nations" (Matt. 28:19). These words have been called the Great Commission and the Church's Marching Orders. In every age since, the church has been called upon to adapt the Great Commission to its own time and place.

In the first chapter of Paul's letter to the Philippians, he speaks of the mission of the church as a *Partnership in the Gospel*—a partnership among Christians and a partnership with God. Paul defines the gospel for us in Romans 1:16: "I am not ashamed of the gospel of Christ for it is the power of God unto salvation." He uses the word "gospel" several times in the first chapter of Philippians. He speaks of **the Confirmation of the Gospel, the Defense of the Gospel,** and **the Advancement of the Gospel.**

By *the Confirmation of the Gospel* Paul means the demonstration of the power of the gospel to change human lives. It is expressed so well in a beautiful sentence in the first chapter of the letter to the Colossians in the Phillips translation: "We also pray that your outward lives, which men may see, may bring credit to your master's name, and that you may bring joy to his heart by bearing genuine fruit, and that your knowledge of God may grow yet deeper" (vv. 9-10).

Paul spent much of his time in *the Defense of the Gospel*. He wrote the letter to the Philippians from a Roman prison cell as he awaited the opportunity to defend the gospel before Caesar himself. He had already defended the gospel before the governors Felix and Festus. In the final chapter of the book of Acts we see Paul in his prison cell defending the gospel before the Jewish leaders of Rome.

In earlier generations it was Christian doctrine that was under attack. Today it is Christian moral values. Later in the letter to the Philippians, Paul reminds us that we are to be "children of God without blemish in the midst of a crooked and perverse generation among whom [we] shine as lights in the world" (Phil. 2:15 RSV).

As the church's greatest missionary, Paul led in *the Advancement of the Gospel*. Wherever Paul went he shared the good news of Christ: in the synagogue, in prison, in the marketplace. He shared the same message with governors and slaves. We have the same obligation. Our mission is, as the motto of Wheaton College, Billy Graham's alma mater: *To Know Christ and to Make Him Known*.

CONSIDERING CHRIST

Wherefore, holy brethren, partakers of the heavenly calling, consider the Apostle and High Priest of our profession, Christ Jesus.

—Hebrews 3:1

Often the minister begins his sermon by saying "I want to consider with you this morning…" and then announces his subject. We find that the invitation to consider is the biblical method of introducing a subject. The psalmist says, "When I consider Thy heavens, the work of Thy fingers, the moon and the stars, which Thou has ordained; what is man that thou art mindful of him?" (8:3-4a). Our Lord said, "Consider the ravens. For they neither sow nor reap; which neither have storehouse nor barn; and yet God feedeth them" (Luke 12:24). And again He said, "Consider the lilies how they grow. They toil not. They spin not; and yet I say to you that Solomon in all his glory was not arrayed like one of these" (Luke 12:27).

But when we come to a consideration of today's subject all other subjects pale into insignificance. Twice in the book of Hebrews we are asked to consider Christ. In 3:1 we read, "Wherefore, holy brethren, partakers of the heavenly calling, consider the Apostle and High Priest of our profession, Christ Jesus." And again in 12:3 we find, "Consider Him that endured such contradiction of sinners against Himself, lest ye be wearied and faint in your minds."

Yes, we consider the lilies of the field, but of far greater importance is it to consider Jesus Christ, the Lily of the Valley. We consider the heavens, the moon and the stars, but how much more important to consider Him, the Bright and Morning Star. Consider Christ Jesus. Consider Him.

It is said that Dannaker, the famous German sculptor, made a bust of Christ which was purchased by Napoleon. As a companion, Napoleon ordered a statue of the pagan goddess Venus. But Dannaker refused, saying, "No man who has had a vision of Christ can desecrate his tools to anything lower." And so if you too will consider Christ and compare Him you will give Him first place in your life.

And so you see of the thousands of words of Scripture the most important are two: consider Him. Consider the Apostle and High Priest of our profession, Christ Jesus. Consider Him who endured such contradiction of sinners. Consider Him.

Have you considered Him? Have you considered Him in your plans? As you lay plans for the future, you must consider Him who has already laid the plans for your future. Consider Him. His plan for your life is the best plan for you.

Have you considered Him? Have you considered Him in your problems? Have you been so troubled with the cares of life that you have failed to appreciate the good things that God gives? Have you been so busy worrying that you have quit praying? Consider Him. Whatever life brings, joy or sorrow, wealth or poverty, success or failure, the question of Christ remains. Have you considered Him?

DENOMINATIONAL DIFFERENCES

There are different kinds of gifts, but the same Spirit.
—1 Corinthians 12:4 NIV

One of the questions that I have often been asked in the over fifty years that I have been in the ministry is, "Why are there so many denominations?" It is certainly a legitimate question. Currently there are nearly three hundred different denominations in our country, most of them purporting to be Christian. This seems to be so contradictory to the emphasis in the New Testament on the unity of the believers.

You can appreciate, then, the experience of the traveling salesman who found himself stranded in a small town in the Midwest on a weekend. He wanted to attend church on Sunday so he asked the desk clerk about the churches in town. The clerk replied, "Well, if you go down to Main Street and First Avenue, you will find the Methodist church on the northwest corner, the Baptist church on the northeast corner, the Presbyterian church on the southwest corner, and the Lutheran church on the southeast corner."

The salesman shook his head and said, "Well, I certainly hope that the dear Lord has a sense of humor."

Now to be sure, differences between Christians can be a hindrance to the work of God. On the other hand, our differences can be an asset in the service of God. P. K. Wrigley once said, "If two people in any organization agree about everything, one of them isn't necessary." Certainly friendly rivalry between denominations or within denominations can be a healthy thing. When someone suggested to Abraham Lincoln that there were too many denominations, he replied, "My good brother, you are all wrong. The more denominations we have the better. They are all getting somebody in that the others could not; and even with the numerous divisions, we are all doing tolerably well."

In 1 Corinthians Paul compares the church to a human body. What he says is that it is the diversity in the church that is its strength. An eye is not an ear. A hand is not a foot. In fact, someone has suggested that the various denominations represent the various parts of the body of Christ. The Episcopalians who emphasize beauty in worship are the eyes of Christ. The Presbyterians who have placed great emphasis on education are the mind of Christ. The Lutherans who have emphasized preaching are the voice of Christ. The Methodists who have shown great concern for the needy are the hands of Christ, And the Baptists who have led in the missionary enterprise are the feet of Christ. As Paul says in 1 Corinthians 12:4, "There are different kinds of gifts, but the same Spirit" (NIV).

GOD'S PSYCHIATRY

For everything in the world—the cravings of sinful man, the lust of his eyes and the boasting of what he has and does—comes not from the Father but from the world.

—1 John 2:16 NIV

In one of his television talks in the award winning series *Life is Worth Living*, Bishop Fulton Sheen discussed the theories of the three founding fathers of the science of psychiatry: Sigmund Freud, Alfred Adler, and Carl Jung. He gave a brief synopsis of each theory and then concluded that each was one-third right. His basis for that conclusion was the words in 1 John 2:16, "For all that is in the world, the lust of the flesh, and the lust of the eyes, and the pride of life, is not of the Father, but is of the world."

Let me share with you some biblical principles that will help you overcome each of these members of the "Trinity of Evil." First, *be filled with the Spirit.* That is the antidote to the lust of the flesh. We should point out that the word "flesh" like the word "world" has more than one meaning in Scripture. Sometimes it refers to our physical bodies, but most often in the epistles of the New Testament it refers to our old sinful nature before we knew Christ.

The antidote for the second member of the Trinity of Evil, the lust of the eye, is the advice given by the apostle Paul to young Timothy: *Be content with such things as you have.* As Paul put it, "Godliness with contentment is great gain. For we brought nothing into the world and we can take nothing out. But if we have food and clothing, we will be content with that" (1 Tim. 6:6-8 NIV).

Finally, the antidote for the pride of life is: *Humble yourself under the mighty hand of God.* Those are the words of the apostle Peter, who learned that lesson well and who needed to learn it well.

During one of Billy Graham's London crusades, a London psychiatrist decided to attend one of the crusade meetings to psychoanalyze Billy Graham and his techniques. As Billy Graham preached the psychiatrist found himself less interested in Billy Graham than in what he was saying. When the invitation was given, he went forward and received Christ as his personal savior. The next morning he went back to his office and told his patients what he had done and invited them to attend the crusade meetings.

What Jesus Christ, the great psychiatrist, did for him, He can do for you and me. For Jesus said, "Whoever comes to me, I will never drive away" (John 6:37b NIV). That is God's psychiatry.

WELL, BLESS MY SOUL

Praise the Lord, O my soul; all my inmost being, praise His holy name.
—Psalm 103:1 NIV

"Well, bless my soul!" That is an expression which we use some-times when we have received some pleasant surprise. In a similar way the psalmist refers to his soul when he considers God's great love for him. In the King James Version Psalm 103:1 reads, "Bless the Lord, O my soul: and all that is within me, bless His holy name." The writer calls upon his soul to bless the Lord because his soul has been so richly blessed by the Lord.

Let us think of how great God's love is. There are a number of places in Psalm 103 that refer to that topic. "For as high as the heavens are above the earth, so great is His love for those who fear him; as far as the east is from the west, so far has he removed our transgressions from us" (vv. 11-12). "From everlasting to everlasting the Lord's love is with those who fear Him" (v. 17a NIV).

But the psalmist uses yet another figure as he contemplates the greatness of God. It is a figure more meaningful than any of the others. "As a father has compassion on his children, so the Lord has compas-sion on those who fear Him" (v. 13 NIV). It is within that concept, the Fatherhood of God, that we can most nearly comprehend the love of God. The Fatherhood of God is essentially a New Testament teaching. The reference in this psalm to God as our Father is but one of two or three in the entire Old Testament, which is three-fourths of the Bible.

It is through the life and ministry of Jesus that we see God revealed to us as a loving heavenly Father. God was His Father. Even His enemies said, "He was even calling God His Father making Himself equal with God" (John 5:18b). It is through Christ that God becomes our Father. The Bible says, "For ye are all the children of God by faith in Christ

Jesus" (Gal. 3:26). Jesus' best known parable, that of the Prodigal Son, illustrates for us in an unforgettable way the love of God our Father for us. And Jesus taught us to pray saying, "Our Father which art in heaven" (Matt. 6:9).

Ultimately it is in the cross that we see the love of God our Father. "For God so loved the world that He gave His only begotten Son that whosoever believeth in Him should not perish but have everlasting life" (John 3:16). And as Paul observes in the Epistle to the Romans, "God demonstrates His own love for us in this: While we were still sinners, Christ died for us" (5:8 NIV).

Perhaps you have seen the plaque that contains these words: "I asked Christ, how much do you love me? And He raised up his arms and died." And that is the measure of God's love.

GONE FISHING

"Come, follow me," Jesus said, "and I will make you fishers of men."
—Matthew 4:19 NIV

One of the symbols of early Christianity was the fish. That seems appropriate since several of the apostles were fishermen. It is said that the symbol was sometimes used as a secret code by the early Christians in that era when Christianity was a crime punishable by death. When a Christian would meet someone and wanted to know if that person was a Christian, he would draw an arc in the sand. If the other person was a Christian, he would draw an arc facing in the opposite direction and intersecting the other arc to form the outline of a fish thus identifying himself as a fellow believer.

Greek was the universal language in the ancient world. The Greek word for fish is *ichthus*. It is an acronym for "Jesus Christ, Son of God." An acronym is a word formed from the initial letters of other words. This is an echo of Peter's great confession. When Peter was asked by Jesus "Who do you say that I am?" he replied "You are the Christ, the Son of the living God" (Matt 16:15-16).

The ultimate identifying mark of the Christian is love. Jesus said to His disciples, "By this all will know that you are my disciples, if you have love for one another" (John 13:35). Even the pagans noticed this. They said, "Behold these Christians how they love another." As a popular Christian song has it, "They will know that we are Christians by our love."

GREAT WORDS OF THE GOSPEL: JUSTIFICATION

Therefore, since we have been justified through faith, we have peace with God through our Lord Jesus Christ.

—Romans 5:1

Justification is that act of God in which the sinner who believes on Christ is declared righteous because of the work of Christ. It is one of the great words of the Bible and Christian theology. Justification by faith is the theme of the Epistle to the Romans, the textbook of Christian theology. Justification by faith was the battle cry of the Protestant Reformation.

The elements of justification are two: remission of punishment and restoration to favor. The penalty for sin is death. For the Bible says, "The soul that sins it shall die" (Ezek. 18:4c) and "The wages of sin is death" (Rom. 6:23). Christ paid the penalty for our sins when He died upon the cross. As Paul says elsewhere in this letter, "God commendeth His love toward us in that while we were yet sinners, Christ died for us" (Rom. 5:8). We receive this benefit when we accept Christ as our Savior.

The other element of justification is restoration to favor, that is, God's favor. Justification is more than remission or acquittal. This would leave the sinner simply in the position of a pardoned criminal. Besides deliverance from punishment, justification implies God's treatment of the sinner as if he were, and had been, personally righteous. As someone has said, "Justified means just as if I had not sinned." These are the outward effects of justification: remission of penalty and restoration to favor.

But justification also has an effect upon our inner life: our attitudes, our emotions, and our values. That is the emphasis in this passage of Scripture. So many of the words that the apostle uses here refer to the inner life: peace, joy, hope, love, character.

333

At the end of World War II General MacArthur received the surrender of the Japanese on board the battleship Missouri, and on that memorable day there was peace between our two nations. In addition, everyone in this country, whether on the battlefront or the home front, experienced an inner peace as a result of that event.

THE MESSAGE OF THE CROSS

For the message of the cross is foolishness to those who are perishing, but to us who are being saved it is the power of God.
—1 Corinthians 1:18 NKJV

There is something rather strange about these words of the apostle Paul. For here he contrasts foolishness with power. It would seem more logical to contrast foolishness with wisdom. Thus, we might read, "The message about the cross is foolishness to those who are perishing, but unto us which are being saved it is the wisdom of God." Or it would seem logical to contrast power with weakness. In that case we would read, "The message of the cross is weakness to those who are perishing, but unto us which are being saved it is the power of God."

As a matter of fact, if we read the context in which 1 Corinthians 1:18 occurs, we see that Paul does contrast foolishness and wisdom and then weakness and power. Verse 25 reads, "for God's foolishness is wiser than human wisdom, and God's weakness is stronger than human strength." In the previous verse Paul speaks of "Christ the power of God and the wisdom of God." Thus, we see that the real meaning of this verse is understood when we say, "The message of the cross is foolishness and weakness to those who are perishing, but unto us which are being saved it is the wisdom and the power of God."

The message of the cross, then, is the essential doctrine of the Christian faith. It is a message to be believed. The message of the cross is also the essential dynamic of the Christian life. It is a message to be lived. The message of the cross is the essential basis of Christian faith and life.

When I served the Lincoln Baptist Church out in Wayne County, we had a discussion group each Sunday following the service. It was led by a Rochester attorney who lived near the church. He would often choose as the basis of the discussion something that I had said

335

in the sermon that morning. Can you imagine being cross-examined by a lawyer about your sermon? Actually, it was a good experience and helpful to me and I hope to others as well. Well, one morning one of the ladies in the group said something to the effect that she objected to people going around saying that they were saved. She said, "You don't know whether you're saved until you die." A number of people in the group objected to that. Usually in such cases of gridlock the leader would turn to the minister and ask for his opinion. Thanks a lot!

Well, in this case I was able to explain that both parties were right. For the New Testament uses the word saved in three different ways regarding our relationship with God. The Bible says that as soon as we believe on Christ we are saved from the *penalty* of sin. It also says that we are being saved from the *power* of sin. As we yield more of ourselves to Christ we are enabled by the Holy Spirit to gain increasing victory over sin in our lives. And some day we shall be saved from the *presence* of sin. For there is no sin in heaven.

THE NEW COMMANDMENT

A new commandment I give unto you, that you love one another, as I have loved you, that you also love one another. By this all will know that you are My disciples, if you have love for one another.

—John 13:34-35

Christian young people today have a chorus which they like to sing: "The Gospel in a Word Is Love." If you had to define or describe the gospel in a single word, the best word to do that would be "love."

This passage of Scripture bears that out. Three times in two verses Jesus says, *"Love one another."* "A new commandment I give you: *Love one another.*" "As I have loved you, so you must *love one another.*" "All men will know that you are my disciples if you love one another." Anything that Jesus repeats three times in two verses is important.

Now this commandment was not accompanied by fire and smoke as was the case when God spoke to Moses on Mt. Sinai. And yet this commandment is authenticated by the life and teachings of our Lord Jesus Christ. He said, "Think not that I come to destroy the law and the prophets. I came not to destroy, but to fulfill" (Matt. 5:17). When asked which was the greatest commandment he replied, "The first and great commandment is: Thou shalt love the Lord thy God with all thy heart and with all thy soul and with all thy mind. And the second is like unto it: Thou shalt love thy neighbor as thyself. On these two laws hang all the laws and the prophets" (Matt. 22:40). And those two commandments hang together. To love God is to love one's neighbor as oneself.

Would you know the sum of all Christian duty and grace? It is this: love one another. There is an ancient tradition about the apostle John, the last of the apostles to die and the only one to die a natural death. After his release from exile on the Isle of Patmos, he returned to Ephesus where a great Christian church existed. Each Sunday, the frail ninety-year-old man was carried into the service where he spoke one sentence to the people, always the same: "Little children, love one another."

Why did Jesus call this a new commandment? Not because He asked us to love one another, for He had already said that: "Thou shalt love thy neighbor." He even said, "Love your enemies." The reason that He called it a new commandment is because of the last part of the verse, which says "as I have loved you." The kind of love that Christ displayed upon the cross is the kind of love that we are to have for each other. Paul said, "Be ye kind, tenderhearted, forgiving one another, even as God for Christ's sake has forgiven you" (Eph. 4:32). That is Christlike love.

THE VISION OF PEACE

In the last days the mountain of the LORD's temple will be established as chief among the mountains; it will be raised above the hills, and all nations will stream to it.

—Isaiah 2:2 NIV

Isaiah is known to us not only as the Prince of the Prophets but also as the Messianic prophet. For he depicts more clearly for us the person and work of the coming Messiah than any other prophet. Isaiah foresaw this prophecy of universal peace being fulfilled in the person of one whom he identified as the Prince of Peace. Christians believe that our Lord Jesus Christ is the Prince of Peace promised by Isaiah. We believe that this promise began to be fulfilled with the birth of Jesus as the angels sang "Peace on earth, good will to men." We believe that its ultimate fulfillment will take place with His second advent when He shall come to judge the nations.

Since Isaiah wrote these words, some twenty-seven hundred years have come and gone and we might very well ask, "Is this promise of peace on earth being fulfilled today?" I think that we can all identify with Henry Wadsworth Longfellow when he wrote:

And in despair I bowed my head
"There is no peace on earth," I said,
"For hate is strong and mocks the song
Of peace on earth, good will to men."

But I think that we must also identify with these later words:

Then pealed the bells more loud and deep
God is not dead nor doth He sleep;

The wrong shall fail, the right prevail,
With peace on earth, good will to men!
("I Heard the Bells on Christmas Day")

It seems to me then that the more important question is not "Is this promise of peace on earth being fulfilled today?" but rather, "How can we help it to be fulfilled today in our world?"

In the Bible peace is a condition of freedom from disturbance, whether outwardly, as of a nation from war or enemies, or inwardly, within the soul. The peace that Christ brought is primarily spiritual peace from and with God, peace in the heart, peace as the disposition of spirit. But, of course, the spirit of the gospel and of the Christian is one of peace, and it is a Christian duty to seek to bring war and strife everywhere to an end. This is represented as the ultimate result of the gospel and Spirit of Christ: universal and permanent peace can only come as the Spirit rules in men's hearts.

So may thy kingdom come in me: may thy will be done in me and on earth as in heaven. For as an old Chinese proverb has it, "When there is righteousness in the heart, there is harmony in the home. When there is harmony in the home, there is order in the nation. When there is order in the nation, there is peace in the world."

THE VOICE OF GOD

The next day John saw Jesus coming toward him, and said, "Behold! The Lamb of God who takes away the sin of the world!"

—John 1:29

"I know not what course others may take, but, as for me; give me liberty or give me death"—Patrick Henry was a voice crying in the wilderness. "A house divided against itself cannot stand"—Abraham Lincoln was a voice crying in the wilderness. "Let us make the world safe for democracy"—Woodrow Wilson was a voice crying in the wilderness. "The only thing that we have to fear is fear itself"—Franklin Roosevelt was a voice crying in the wilderness. "Ask not what your country can do for you; ask what you can do for your country"—John F. Kennedy was a voice crying in the wilderness.

In every age there have been such voices crying in the wilderness and remembered by one brief sentence. John the Baptist described himself as a voice crying in the wilderness. His one sentence are the words found in John 1:29, "Behold the Lamb of God who takes away the sin of the world." John had but one brief sentence to utter in the play upon the stage of life. But that one sentence is the message of the Christian faith. It has changed the course of human history as has no other word. It can change your life and mine.

I never think of these words of John the Baptist without thinking of an experience from the life of Charles Spurgeon, the great English preacher. Early in his ministry his congregation erected a new building seating five thousand people, the first Metropolitan Tabernacle. The Saturday afternoon before he was to preach in the new church for the first time he went into the sanctuary to try out his voice in this great building. He stood behind the pulpit where he was to preach so often and cried out in the words of John the Baptist, "Behold the Lamb of God that taketh away the sin of the world." Away up in the balcony, a carpenter was putting some finishing touches to the last row of pews. When he heard these words he was so smitten with a sense of his own sin and his need of the Savior that he laid down his hammer and went home where he knelt beside his bed and gave his heart and life to Jesus Christ.

> If I were a voice—a persuasive voice—
> That could travel the wide world through
> I would fly on the beam of the morning light
> And speak to men with a gentle might
> And tell them to be true.
> I'd fly, I'd fly o'er land and sea,
> Wherever a human heart might be
> Telling a tale, or singing a song,
> In praise of the right—in blame of the wrong.

THE WAY EVERLASTING

See if there be any wicked way in me, and lead me in the way everlasting.

—Psalm 139:24

Nowhere are the great attributes of God—His omniscience, His omnipotence, His omnipresence—set forth so strikingly as they are in this magnificent psalm. The psalm consists of four stanzas of six verses each. The first stanza deals with God's omniscience—the fact that God knows everything. The second stanza confirms that God is everywhere at the same time—He is omnipresent. The third stanza is related to God's omnipotence. Nowhere is God's unlimited power seen more clearly than in His creation.

The fourth stanza is the Psalmist's appropriation and application of these great truths to his own heart and life. It is one thing to believe in the omniscience of God—the fact that God knows everything—and quite another thing to believe that God knows all about you. It is one thing to believe in the omnipresence of God and quite another thing to believe that He is with you at all times. It is one thing to believe in the omnipotence of God and quite another thing to believe that God can do all things in your behalf.

Thus, the psalm concludes with a beautiful prayer which I trust will be your petition and mine as we listen for the voice of God: "Search me, O God, and know my heart; Try me and know my thoughts. See if there be any wicked way in me and lead me in the way everlasting."

When I was a student at Northern Baptist Seminary I remember a series of chapel talks by Irish evangelist J. Edwin Orr. In one of his talks he told of a day when he was sitting alone in a park in Australia while on a preaching mission. As he was meditating, the words of Psalm 139 came to mind and in fifteen minutes he composed the words to a beautiful hymn. It was his prayer that day. May it be yours and mine.

Search me, O God, and know my heart today;
Try me, O Savior, know my thoughts I pray.
See if there be some wicked way in me;
Cleanse me from every sin and set me free.

Lord, take my life, and make it wholly Thine;
Fill my poor heart with Thy great love divine.
Take all my will, my passion, self and pride;
I now surrender, Lord, in me abide.

TREASURES OF WISDOM

Blessed is the man who finds wisdom, the man who gains understanding.

—Proverbs 3:13 NIV

Wisdom, as that term is used in the Bible, may be defined as a realistic approach to the problems of life, including all the practical skills and the technical arts of civilization. It falls into two classes, which have their counterparts in Egyptian and Babylonian wisdom as well: lower or practical wisdom, and higher or speculative wisdom.

The principal goal of the lower or practical wisdom was to teach young men how to cultivate the personal qualities needed to achieve success and avoid failure. Practical wisdom was the most secular branch of Israelite intellectual activity. It was practical in its goals and realistic in its assessment of human nature. It was rational in its approach, being based on observation and common sense rather than on the tradition of the priests or the revelation of the prophets.

In addition to the lower or practical wisdom of the Hebrews there was also the higher or speculative wisdom. Among the many teachers of wisdom were some who sought to penetrate to the great abiding issues of life—the meaning of existence, the purpose of creation, the nature of death, the problem of suffering.

It seems to me that these ought to be the concerns of educated people. An education should not only prepare a person to earn a living, it should also teach one how to live. On one occasion at Harvard, Emerson commented to Henry Thoreau on the progress of the university, "Harvard now has all of the branches of learning." To which Thoreau replied, "But none of the roots." In addition to teaching people to avoid failure and achieve success, an education should prepare one to deal with the ultimate issues of life.

Perhaps there is no better illustration of these things than the experience of C. S. Lewis, late Professor of Medieval and Renaissance Literature at Oxford and Cambridge Universities. One night in his room at Oxford, he knelt down in prayer and admitted that God was God. That was only the beginning, but as one of his contemporaries who knew him most of his life said, "C. S. Lewis was the most converted man I ever knew." His conversion bore fruit, for in a few short years he became the most able and articulate defender of the Christian faith in modern times. For he had discovered what the apostle Paul meant when he spoke of "the mystery of God, namely, Christ, in whom are hidden all the treasures of wisdom and knowledge" (Col. 2:2b-3 NIV).

A GOOD SOLDIER OF JESUS CHRIST

Endure hardship…like a good soldier of Christ Jesus.

—2 Timothy 2:3

Tom Convery was the platoon sergeant for 4th Platoon, Company E, 397th Infantry Regiment, 100th Infantry Division. As such it fell as his unhappy lot to be my platoon sergeant. Tom was older than most of the men in the company—all of thirty-five. He didn't always have a lot of patience with teenage soldiers like myself. One day in November 1944, our platoon was bedding down for the night in a house near the Maginot Line. Tom saw me folding my raincoat to make a pillow against the stone floor. (You were supposed to sleep with your helmet on.) He shook his head sadly and said, "Nemecek, you'll never be a soldier." As a smart-mouthed teenager, I was very quick to point out that I never wanted to be a soldier in the first place.

Six months later, April 5, 1945, our division was attacking the city of Heilbronn, Germany, in house-to-house fighting. Early that morning the building was set on fire under a heavy German counterattack. Sgt. Convery ordered our platoon and part of another to withdraw. Of the thirty men in the building at the time, six were killed and many others wounded. As Sgt. Convery was being carried on a stretcher to the Battalion Aid Station, he apologized to the Company Commander for not being able to hold the position! Years later while thinking about that incident, as I have done thousands of times since, I remembered the words of the apostle Paul, "Endure hardship as a good soldier of Jesus Christ."

Paul knew a great deal about both of these things, *soldiers* and *hardship*. He was often guarded by Roman soldiers and would soon know the details of their personal lives. There are references in nearly all of Paul's letters to military life. In fact, he wrote his own epitaph in this

347

metaphor. "I have fought the good fight, I have finished the race, I have kept the faith" (2 Tim. 4:7).

Paul defended his apostleship in his first letter to the Corinthians by pointing to the hardships which he had endured in the cause of Christ:

I have worked much harder. Been in prison more frequently, been flogged more severely and been exposed to death again and again. Five times I received from the Jews the forty lashes minus one. Three times I was beaten with rods, once I was stoned, three times I was shipwrecked. I spent a night and a day in the open sea. I have been constantly on the move. I have been in danger from rivers, in danger from bandits, in danger from my own countrymen, in danger from Gentiles, in danger in the city, in danger in the country, in danger at sea; and in danger from false brothers. I have labored and toiled and have often gone without sleep; I have known hunger and thirst and have often gone without food; I have been cold and naked. Besides everything else, I face daily the pressure of my concern for all the churches. (2 Cor. 11:23b-28)

What was the source of Sgt. Convery's strength? He was a praying man. On March 15, 1945, our division began the offensive that would take us over the Rhine and into the heart of Germany. Early that morning our entire regiment passed through a French village. The enemy had been waiting for us all winter and they were ready. Artillery, rockets, and mortar fire pounded down on us. Standing in the middle of the main street of the deserted town was Father O'Brien, the Regimental Chaplain. Stepping out of the line of march, men would go up to him to receive his blessing. Among those was Sgt. Tom.

Stand up, stand up for Jesus, The trumpet call obey;
Forth to the mighty conflict In this His glorious day;
Ye that are men, now serve Him Against unnumbered foes;
Let courage rise with danger, And strength to strength oppose.

Stand up, stand up for Jesus, The strife will not be long;
This day the noise of battle, the next, the victor's song:
To Him that overcometh a crown of life shall be
He with the King of glory Shall reign eternally.
(George Duffield, "Stand Up, Stand Up for Jesus")

WHAT IS MARRIAGE?

Wives, submit yourselves unto your own husbands, as unto the Lord.
—Ephesians 5:22

The central issue in marriage is how two distinct personalities can, in the words of Scripture, "become one flesh." Ogden Nash, the American humorist, had an article many years ago in *The Saturday Evening Post* entitled "A Definition of Marriage." He said, "I know that marriage is a legal and religious alliance entered into by a man who can't sleep with the window shut and a woman who can't sleep with the window open." He then gives several other such examples and concludes, "That is why marriage is so much more interesting than divorce, because it's the only known example of the happy meeting of the immovable object and the irresistible force. So I hope husbands and wives will continue to debate and combat over everything debatable and combatable, because I believe a little incompatibility is the spice of life, particularly if he has income and she is patable."

The apostle Paul addressed this issue of the blending of personalities in marriage in a famous passage in Ephesians chapter 5. It is the passage that contains the words, "Wives, submit yourselves unto your own husbands as unto the Lord" (v. 22). This verse has been given a number of misinterpretations. One of them is the male chauvinist interpretation represented by Ralph Cramden of the *Honeymooners* who said in the midst of a heated argument with his wife, "Remember, I'm the boss. You're nothing." His wife replied, "Big deal. You're the boss of nothing!" So much for the macho man view of marriage.

There is also the female chauvinist view of this verse. It says that the wife is really the head of the house but she lets her husband think that he is. One husband explained it this way: "When we were married my wife and I agreed that I would make all of the big decisions and she would make all of the little decisions. After a few years I discovered that a little decision is whether or not to buy a new house or a new car and a big decision is whether or not to admit Red China to the United Nations."

The reason that this passage in Ephesians is so often misunderstood is because people begin reading at the wrong place. It does not begin with the admonition, "Wives, submit yourselves unto your husbands" but rather with the previous verse which says, "Submit yourselves one to another in godly fear" (v. 21). As Charles E. Fuller of the Old Fashioned Revival Hour used to say, "Marriage is not a fifty-fifty proposition. It must be at least a sixty-forty one." That is, each partner going more than halfway. In the Ephesians passage Paul goes on to say, "Wives, submit yourselves unto your husbands as unto the Lord." Later on he addresses the husband, "Husbands, love your wives even as Christ loved the church and gave himself for it" (v. 25). There he is speaking of the cross. Here then is the formula for a perfect marriage. If you will give me a wife who will submit herself unto her husband as though he were God Himself and a husband who loves his wife so much that he is willing to die for her, I will guarantee that you will have what God intended that a marriage should be: a little bit of heaven on earth.

THE SEVEN DEADLY SINS

*Here is a trustworthy saying that deserves full acceptance: Christ Jesus
came into the world to save sinners...*

—1 Timothy 1:15 NIV

I am sure that you are familiar with the Seven Danger Signals of
Cancer announced by the American Cancer Society. By way of review
they are: (1) Any sore that does not heal; (2) A lump or thickening in
the breast or elsewhere; (3) Unusual bleeding or discharge; (4) Any
change in a wart or mole; (5) Persistent indigestion or difficulty in
swallowing; (6) Persistent hoarseness or cough; (7) Any change in
normal bowel habits.

But are you familiar with the seven dangers of the soul? They are
called the Seven Deadly Sins. It was Pope Gregory the Great who gave
them their present form and name: pride, covetousness, lust, anger,
gluttony, envy, sloth. It is interesting to note that James, who lived
several centuries before Gregory, deals with all seven in his epistle.

Pride—"But He giveth more grace. Wherefore He saith. 'God
resisteth the proud, but giveth grace unto the humble'" (4:6).

Covetousness—"Ye ask, and receive not, because ye ask amiss, that
ye may consume it upon your lusts" (4:3). "Your gold and silver is
cankered; and the rust of them shall be a witness against you, and
shall eat your flesh as it were fire. Ye have heaped treasure together
for the last days" (5:3).

Lust—"From whence come wars and fightings among you? Come
they not hence, even of your lusts that war in your members?"
(4:1). "Ye ask, and receive not, because ye ask amiss, that ye may
consume it upon your lusts" (4:3).

Anger—"Ye kill, and desire to have, and cannot obtain" (4:2b).

Gluttony—"Ye have lived in pleasure on the earth, and been wanton; ye have nourished your hearts, as in a day of slaughter" (5:5).

Envy—"Do ye think that the scripture saith in vain, The spirit that dwelleth in us lusteth to envy?" (4:5).

Sloth—"Therefore to him that knoweth to do good, and doeth it not, to him it is sin" (4:17).

Do you know that you have committed the seven deadly sins? The Bible says, "All have sinned and come short of the glory of God" (Rom. 3:23), and "For whosoever shall keep the whole law and yet offend in one point is guilty of all" (James 2:10). Do you know that you can be forgiven? Jesus told of two men who went to the temple to pray. One told God that he had kept the whole law. Actually he had committed the worst of the seven deadly sins—pride. The second man simply prayed, "God be merciful to me a sinner" (Luke 18:13). Jesus said it was this second man who went to his house justified rather than the other.

THE PILGRIM'S SONG

The LORD will watch over your coming and going both now and forevermore.

—Psalm 121:8 NIV

Psalm 121 has been called the "Traveler's Psalm," no doubt because of the beautiful promise in the final verse: "The Lord will watch over your coming and going both now and forevermore." This Psalm was apparently sung by the pilgrims who traveled from various regions of Israel to attend the sacred feasts in Jerusalem. Jerusalem is set on a series of hills, and thus the psalm begins, "I will lift up my eyes unto the hills from whence comes my help. My help comes from the Lord who made heaven and earth" (vv. 1-2). The Israelites believed that God dwelt in a very special way in the temple in Jerusalem and that He alone was the maker of heaven and earth.

Many another pilgrim has found comfort and strength in the words of this beautiful song. When David Livingstone left the little village of Blantyre in Scotland for missionary service in Africa, both he and his parents realized that they would never see each other again in this life. So it was, that in their last moments together Livingstone's father took the family Bible and read to his son this psalm and offered a prayer that its promises might apply to his son as he set sail for the dark continent in the Lord's service.

David Livingstone found those promises to be true. Years later, when he had become world famous, he returned to Scotland and spoke to the students at the University of Glasgow. He paused in the middle of his address and asked the students, "Would you like to know what it was that sustained me in the midst of the loneliness and deprivation of those many months in the heart of Africa? It was the promise of the Savior, 'Lo, I am with you always, even to the end of the world'" (Matt. 28:20b).

355

Now you may never make a pilgrimage to Jerusalem or serve as a missionary to Africa, but let me assure you that your life is a pilgrimage and these promises are for you in your daily walk. Dr. E. Stanley Jones, the famous missionary and devotional writer, entitled his autobiography *A Song of Ascents*. For, you see, he saw his life as a pilgrimage through this world to that New Jerusalem where there is no temple, for the Lord God Himself is the temple there. You and I are on that same pilgrimage. We, too, have the assurance that the Maker of Heaven and Earth, the Keeper of Israel, and the Lover of our Souls is our helper whatever the journey may bring. So, as we go, may we sing the glad songs of Zion. For remember, life is not a burden to be borne but a song to be sung.

THE TRANSFORMED LIFE

Therefore if any man be in Christ, he is a new creature: old things are passed away; behold, all things are become new.

—2 Corinthians 5:17

In Mark 9 we read, "After six days Jesus took Peter, James and John with him and led them up a high mountain, where they were all alone. There he was transfigured before them" (vv. 2-3). The word which is translated "transfigured" here is a Greek word which is the basis of our English word "*metamorphosis*." In zoology metamorphosis is the word that is used to describe the process by which the larvae of a cocoon is changed into a butterfly. At the transfiguration our Lord put off for a moment the form of his true humanity and displayed only the beauty of his true divinity.

The most general use of the word metamorphosis in English is to describe a striking alteration in appearance, character, or circumstances. In the Gospels the word is used of the transfiguration of Jesus to describe the striking alteration in His appearance. The Greek word is used four times in the New Testament. It is used in Matthew and Mark to describe the transfiguration of our Lord. It is used twice by the apostle Paul in his epistles. Once it is translated "transformed" and once it is translated "changed."

In 1 Corinthians 3:18 Paul describes the change wrought in us when Christ enters our lives. "But we all, with open face beholding as in a glass the glory of the Lord, are changed into the same image from glory to glory, even as by the Spirit of the Lord." Paul used the word again in his great challenge to Christian commitment in Romans 12:1-2: "I beseech you, brethren, by the mercies of God that you present our bodies as living sacrifices; holy, acceptable unto God; which is your reasonable service and be not conformed to the world, but be ye transformed by the renewing of your mind that you may prove what is that good, and acceptable and perfect will of God." That is the Christian's Mount of Transfiguration.

We do not understand the miracle of the transfiguration unless we see in it the power of Christ to change human life. In Raphael's great painting *The Transfiguration,* we have magnificent portraits of Jesus talking with Moses and Elijah. But at the bottom of the work, at the feet of Jesus, are the figures of the epileptic boy and his father waiting for Jesus to come down from the mountain and heal the child. This is the message of the transfiguration. The same power that transformed the human Jesus into the divine Christ in that moment can work any change in any human heart and life. We need only come to Him as the father of the epileptic boy and cry out with tears, "Lord, I now believe, help thou my unbelief." No person who has been to the mountaintop with Peter and James and John and has seen the glory of Christ can ever be the same. "For if anyone is in Christ, there is a new creation; old things are passed away, behold; all things are become new."

GRANDFATHER'S DAY

Be imitators of God, therefore, as dearly loved children and live a life of love, just as Christ loved us and gave himself up for us as a fragrant offering and sacrifice to God.

—Ephesians 5:1-2 NIV

Art Linkletter was right: "Kids say the darndest things." One first grade teacher was preparing her class for Grandfather's Day. She went around the class asking each student what his or her grandfather did for a living. One little boy whose grandfather was a minister couldn't remember the word for pastor and said, "My grandfather is God."

Dr. W. Robert Smith, professor of philosophy at Bethel College in St. Paul, Minnesota, said in an interview with *Christian Life* magazine, "We live in the place of our Lord in reference to our children." In his letter to the Ephesians, the apostle Paul wrote, "Be imitators of God as little children" (Eph. 5:1).

Not everyone agrees. One lady suggested to her minister that he not offer prayer to God the Father because some people in the congregation will have had a bad relation with their father and would be "turned off." Apparently, Jesus didn't know that. When the disciples asked Him to teach them to pray He said, "After this manner therefore pray, Our Father, which art in heaven" (Matt. 6:9a).

Apparently Harry Johnson didn't know this either. He told me once that his last memory of his father was the beating he gave his mother. Did it affect Harry? Yes, it did. He started a Sunday school for children in a government housing project!

Lord, speak to me that I may speak
In living echoes of Thy tone;
As Thou hast sought, so let me seek
Thy erring children lost and lone.

O fill me with Thy fullness, Lord,
Until my very heart o'er-flow
In kindling thought and glowing word,
Thy love to tell, Thy praise to show.
(Frances R. Havergal, "Lord, Speak to Me")

PRAYING THROUGH

Ask and it will be given to you; seek and you will find; knock and the door will be opened to you.

—Luke 11:9 NIV

Someone has said that there are two kinds of Christians: those who pray without ceasing and those who cease without praying. Certainly Jesus taught us the importance of prayer in the life of a Christian. He taught us by His example. It was while He was in the very act of praying that His disciples said to Him, "Lord, teach us to pray" (Luke 11:1b). Moreover, He encouraged us to pray by the many promises that He gave us regarding prayer. The words of Luke 11:9 are among the greatest of these.

Jesus taught us not only that we should pray, but that we should pray effectively. In this great prayer promise we are taught how to pray. We are to ask. We are to seek. And we are to knock. We are also told that if we pray aright, our prayers will be effective. We will receive. We will find. Doors will be opened to us. The Parable of a Friend at Midnight and this promise which is its moral teach us that we are to persist in sincere and earnest prayer believing that God will hear and answer us.

The classic work on prayer and faith, in my opinion, is *Hudson Taylor's Spiritual Secret.* Hudson Taylor's spiritual secret was just two words: Trust God. Hudson Taylor did that as very few people ever have. He was the founder and director of the China Inland Mission. Hudson Taylor had a very unusual way of praying. He literally prayed upon the basis of the promises of God. If he needed five missionaries for some remote province of China, he would look up one of these great promises regarding prayer and ask God for what he needed. Then, in the margin of his Bible beside the promise, he would write the nature of his request and the date that he offered his petition. When the answer came, as it inevitably did, he would note in the same place when and how the answer came. His Bible was a case record book of answered prayer.

This is the point. In the forty years that he served as director of the China Inland Mission, he never asked anyone to contribute money to the society or asked anyone to volunteer his services for the mission. Yet, in those forty years the China Inland Mission became one of the largest missionary societies in the world. He simply asked and God provided. Have faith in God.

Adoniram Judson, who lived a life of prayer as a missionary to Burma, gave this testimony near the end of his life. He said, "I was never deeply interested in any subject; I never prayed sincerely and earnestly for anything but that it came at some time. No matter how distant the day, somehow, in some shape, probably the last I should have advised, it came."

So then, keep on asking and you will keep on getting; keep on seeking and you will keep on finding; keep on knocking and the door will be opened. "Pray without ceasing"(1 Thess. 5:17).

STRENGTH THROUGH BROKENNESS

And He [Jesus] said unto me, "My grace is sufficient for thee: for my strength is made perfect in weakness." Therefore, most gladly I will rather boast in my infirmities, that the power of Christ may rest upon me.
— 2 Corinthians 12:9

My brother, Ivan, taught in the College of Engineering at the University of Kansas for thirty-two years. His specialties were thermodynamics and heat transfer. One interesting phenomenon that he pointed out from his studies in those areas was the fact that when a broken piece of metal is welded back together that the welded piece is stronger than the original unbroken piece. There is a principle there that applies to much of life. The apostle Paul wrote, "My strength is made perfect in weakness" (2 Cor 12:9).

There is no better example of that principle than the man who wrote those words. In his second letter to the Corinthians Paul speaks of his brokenness: "Five times I received from the Jews the forty lashes minus one. Three times I was beaten with rods, Once I was stoned, three times I was shipwrecked....I have labored and toiled and gone without sleep; I have known hunger and thirst and gone without food; I have been cold and naked" (2 Cor. 11:25, 27).

In addition to these things Paul suffered an incurable affliction which he called his "thorn in the flesh" (2 Cor. 12:7). He prayed three times that God would relieve him of this affliction, but instead God said, "My grace is sufficient for thee; for my strength is made perfect in weakness." The welded piece is stronger than the original unbroken piece!

A little boy was trying to move a large rock in the yard of his home without success. His father asked him, "Are you using all your strength?"

Somewhat exasperated by the question the boy answered, "Of course, I am."
The father replied, "No, you aren't. You haven't asked me to help."
Remember,

"When I am weak,
then I am strong."

THE SHADOW
OF THE ALMIGHTY

They [His angels] will lift you up in their hands, so that you will not strike your foot against a stone.

—Psalm 91:12 NIV

A certain insurance company has as its logo an open umbrella. The implication of that symbol is that all those who are insured by that company are safe from the financial disaster that can result from the perils of life on this planet. The author of the Ninety-first Psalm sees God as his protection from the perils themselves. "He that dwells in the secret place of the most High shall abide under the shadow of the Almighty. I will say of the Lord, He is my refuge and my fortress; my God, in Him will I trust" (vv. 1-2). Then he proceeds to outline in very specific detail all the things from which God will protect him.

It is helpful to read the particular promises in a modern language translation if for no other reason than that the newness of the language impresses these familiar truths upon our minds. For example, in the Good News Bible we are told, "He will keep you safe from all hidden dangers and from all deadly diseases. You need not fear any dangers at night or sudden attacks during the day or the plagues that strike in the dark or the evils that kill in daylight. No disaster will strike you, no violence will come near your home." No insurance company in the world writes a policy like that!

Let me share with you a testimony to these things from a man whom we all knew and loved—Jimmy Stewart. As you may know, Jimmy was the leader of a squadron of B-24 bombers in Europe during World War II. One night at his base in England he found himself overwhelmed by fear as he contemplated another bombing mission over Germany. At that point he took out a letter which his father had sent just before Jimmy went overseas. His father assured him of his prayers and enclosed a copy of the Ninety- first Psalm.

Jimmy read the Psalm again. "I will say of the Lord, He is my refuge and my fortress…His truth shall be my shield and buckler. Thou shalt not be afraid for the terror by night; nor for the arrow that flies by day…He shall give His angels charge over thee, to keep thee in all thy ways. They shall bear thee up in their arms, lest thou dash thy foot against a stone."

"They shall bear thee up in their arms." What a promise for an airman! There on the creaking cot with the night pressing in, I read those comforting words as a prayer. Then I relinquished to the Lord my fears for the coming day. I placed in His hands the squadron I would be leading. And, as the Psalm promised, I felt myself borne up.

I had no illusions about the mission that was coming up. I knew very well what might happen. I had done all I could. I had faced each fear and handed it over to God. And now, no matter what might happen, I knew that He would be with me, in this world or the next.

TURNING THE OTHER CHEEK

If someone strikes you on the right cheek, turn to him the other also.
—Matthew 5:39b

One of the criticisms that people sometimes make about the teachings of Jesus is that they are too idealistic and impractical. I remember seeing a cartoon that depicted a minister standing outside the door of the church greeting the congregation as the people came out of the church. The outdoor sign indicated that he had just preached on the subject "Love Your Neighbor." A matronly lady was standing in front of him wagging her finger under his nose and saying, "I just wish you had my neighbors."

It was Lord Chesterton who said, "Christianity has not failed. It has never really been tried." There have been some instances when the teachings of Jesus have proven to be the solution to some great social problem. Nonviolent resistance as practiced by Gandhi and Martin Luther King and their followers are examples of the teaching of Jesus in the Sermon on the Mount, 'Whoever smites you on the right cheek, turn to him the other also" (Matt. 5:39).

Lest you think that the principle applies only to mass social movements, let me tell you about a man who uses that same principle in the business world—where the tire meets the road. Chet Blue is the owner and manager of the Overhead Door Company of Rochester. Like every businessman, occasionally he has a customer complain about the size of his bill. When that happens, Chet goes over the bill to make sure that there has been no mistake. If there is none, he says to the customer, "That is the correct amount for the work that we did, but if you don't think that it's fair, pay me what you think is fair." In thirty years in the business he has never had a customer refuse to pay the original amount!

Dr. James T. Fisher, in a book entitled *A Few Buttons Missing: The Casebook of a Psychiatrist*, wrote, "If you were to take the sum total of all the authoritative articles ever written by the most qualified of psychologists and psychiatrists on the subject of mental hygiene, if you were to combine them and refine them and cleave out the excess verbiage, if you were to take the whole of the meat and none of the parsley, and if you were to have these unadulterated bits of pure scientific knowledge concisely expressed by the most capable of living poets, you would have an awkward and incomplete summation of the Sermon on the Mount."

WHAT ON EARTH ARE YOU DOING, FOR HEAVEN'S SAKE?

Why do you stand looking up toward heaven?

—Acts 1:11b

It has been said that there are some people who are so heavenly minded that they are no earthly good. That was a concern of our Lord for His disciples following His ascension into heaven. For immediately after he had been taken up, two men in white robes stood by the disciples and asked, "Men of Galilee, why do you stand looking up toward heaven? This Jesus, who has been taken up from you into heaven, will come in the same way as you saw him go into heaven" (Acts 1:11).

By virtue of his resurrection Jesus Christ is Lord of lords and King of kings. There is a natural temptation to assume that He will establish His rule over the world by His own effort. On the day of the ascension the disciples asked that very question: "Lord, is this the time when you will restore the kingdom to Israel?" (Acts 1:6b). But Jesus replied, "You will receive power when the Holy Spirit comes on you; and you will be my witnesses" (Acts 1:8a NIV). It is we, the servants of the Lord, who are to establish His kingdom on earth.

If we believe, as the Scriptures teach, that Christ may return to earth at any time to establish His kingdom, how are we to conduct our lives? The Scriptures tell us that we are to wait on the Lord. That does not mean that we are to stand looking up to heaven. It means that we are to serve the Lord knowing that the final outcome is assured. As someone has suggested, "We are to plan as though Christ were not coming for a thousand years, but we are to live as though he is coming today."

Dr. Carl Lundquist served for thirty years as the president of Bethel College and Seminary in St. Paul, Minnesota. In those thirty years he saw the college grow from an enrollment of forty students to over two thousand, and the seminary from fifty students to over two hundred. Dr. Lundquist led both schools in the move to a new campus and the construction of dozens of new buildings. He revealed, I believe, the secret of his success as an administrator when he talked one day about his student days at Sioux Falls College. He had a little motto that he kept above the light switch in his dormitory room so that he could see it whenever he left his room. It consisted of just two words: "Perhaps Today."

The motivation of the lives of many of God's greatest servants has been the realization that Christ could return at any time. Dr. G. Campbell Morgan, late pastor of the Westminster Chapel in London and one of the great Bible teachers of the last century, once said, "I never begin a sermon without thinking that before I finish, Christ may come and end my work and begin His own."

HOW TO HAVE A HAPPY HOME

Unless the LORD builds the house, its builders labor in vain.
—Psalm 127:1a NIV

On one occasion Frank Lloyd Wright, the noted architect, was conducting a seminar on home construction for a group of professional architects. One of the group asked, "What is the best foundation for a home?" Mr. Wright replied, "A happily married couple."

So says the apostle Paul. In Ephesians 5 he discusses the Christian home and begins with an explanation of the relationship between husbands and wives. "Wives, submit yourselves unto your own husbands as unto the Lord" (v. 22). Some have taken these words to mean that the husband is the lord of the manor and the wife must be the humble and obedient servant of her husband. Ralph Cramden of the *Honeymooners* articulated that view when he said to his wife in the midst of a heated argument, "Remember, I'm the boss; you're nothing." Alice replied, "Big deal! You're the boss of nothing." So much for the macho man view of marriage.

The opposite view is that the wife is the head of the household but she lets her husband think that he is. One husband explained it this way: "When we were first married my wife and I agreed that I would make all of the big decisions and she would make all of the little decisions. After a few years I discovered that a little decision was whether or not to buy a new car or a new home. A big decision was whether or not to admit Red China to the United Nations."

What Paul really teaches is the equality of husband and wife in the marriage relationship. For the passage begins with this admonition, "Submitting yourselves one to another in the fear of God" (v. 21). As Saint Augustine said, "God did not take woman from man that she might be beneath him but from the side of man that they might be equals."

The question then arises, "But who is in charge?" Paul answers, "The Lord himself." "Wives, submit yourselves unto your own husbands *as unto the Lord.*" "Husbands, love your wives *even as Christ* also loved the church and gave himself for it" (v. 25). Give me a wife who submits herself unto her husband as unto the Lord and a husband who is willing to die for his wife even as Christ died for the church and I will guarantee a happy marriage. The late Archbishop Sheen put it well in a television talk entitled "Three to Get Married." A husband, a wife, and the Lord. The formula for a happy home.

SCRIPTURE INDEX

Printed in the United States
203387BV00003B/1-75/P